The Traveler's Guide
to the PONY EXPRESS TRAIL

by
Joe Bensen

FALCON™

Falcon Press® Publishing Co., Inc.
Helena, Montana

Falcon Press is continually expanding its list of recreational guidebooks. All books include detailed descriptions, accurate maps, and all the information necessary for enjoyable trips. You can order extra copies of this book and get information and prices for other Falcon books by writing to Falcon Press Publishing Co., Inc., P.O. Box 1718, Helena, MT 59624. Also, please ask for a free copy of our current catalog lising all Falcon Press books.

Library of Congress Cataloging-in-Publication Data

Bensen, Joe, 1949
        The traveler's guide to the Pony Express trail/by Joe Bensen
                p. cm.
            ISBN 1-56044-233-6
                1. Pony Express Trail—Guidebooks.   I. Title
F590.3.B46   1995
917.804'33—dc20   95-8232
                                                                                    CIP

Falcon Press Publishing Co., Inc.
P.O. Box 1718, Helena, MT 59624

 Text pages printed on recycled paper.

ACKNOWLEDGMENTS

I would like to express my gratitude to the many people who assisted me in my work on this project, from the various state historical society staff who helped answer my many research questions to the folks in small towns along the route who helped me stay on track. I would especially like to thank Joe Nardone, historian, writer, and Pony Express expert, *sans pareil*, for generously sharing both his extensive knowledge of the route and his great enthusiasm for the subject. I would also like to thank Jacqueline Lewin, history curator of the St. Joseph Museum, and Larry Carpenter, secretary of the National Pony Express Association, for their very helpful feedback on my manuscript.

Of the many folks who showed me great kindness along the way, who gave me directions, fixed my flat tires, let me enter their private property, and generally made my drives more productive and enjoyable, I would like to single out Duane Durst, guide and caretaker at Hollenberg Ranch, and David Rosen, naturalist and park ranger with California State Parks.

Finally, I would be remiss were I not to acknowledge the hard work of my old friend, climbing partner, and editor on this project, Randall Green—a paragon of patience!

CONTENTS

Marker for Kennekuk Station, Kansas.

FOREWORD

The story of the Pony Express represents one of the most romantic chapters in the history of the American West. For a brief period in 1860-1861, an elite group of daring young couriers raced the 1,966 miles between St. Joseph, Missouri, and Sacramento, California, relaying mail and telegraph messages in as little as ten days—less than half the time of the previous fastest delivery. The Express riders carried 34,753 pieces of mail across what was the most desolate and dangerous terrain in North America. They rode non-stop through day and night, pausing only to switch horses and relay their pouches from rider to rider at carefully spaced stations.

With the completion of the transcontinental telegraph line, in October of 1861, the short run of the Pony Express came to an end. But thanks to the popular press of the time, the exploits of the Express riders became a legendary part of the story of the Wild West. Today that legend is kept alive by movies and television, and by the many restored historic sites along the original Pony Express route, attractions that continue to capture the imaginations of so many vacation travelers.

PONY EXPRESS TRAIL

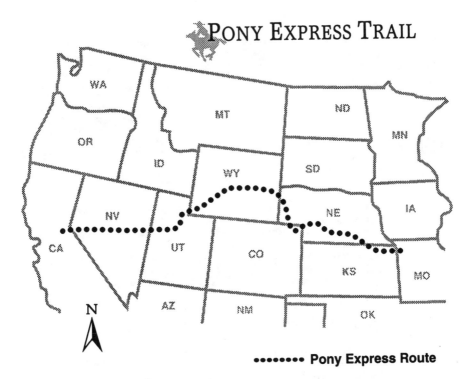

•••••••• **Pony Express Route**

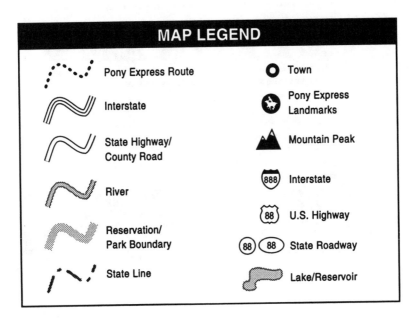

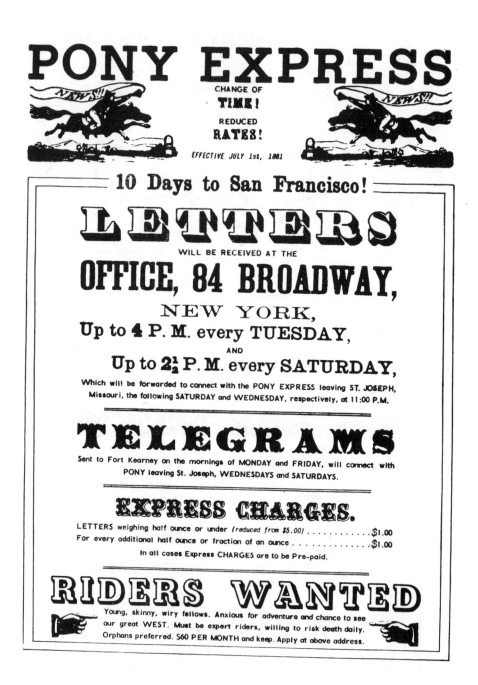

PONY EXPRESS

CHANGE OF
TIME!
REDUCED
RATES!

EFFECTIVE JULY 1st, 1861

10 Days to San Francisco!

LETTERS

WILL BE RECEIVED AT THE

OFFICE, 84 BROADWAY,

NEW YORK,

Up to **4** P. M. every TUESDAY,

AND

Up to **2½** P. M. every SATURDAY,

Which will be forwarded to connect with the PONY EXPRESS leaving ST. JOSEPH,
Missouri, the following SATURDAY and WEDNESDAY, respectively, at 11:00 P.M.

TELEGRAMS

Sent to Fort Kearney on the mornings of MONDAY and FRIDAY, will connect with
PONY leaving St. Joseph, WEDNESDAYS and SATURDAYS.

EXPRESS CHARGES.

LETTERS weighing half ounce or under (reduced from $5.00) $1.00
For every additional half ounce or fraction of an ounce $1.00
In all cases Express CHARGES are to be Pre-paid.

RIDERS WANTED

Young, skinny, wiry fellows. Anxious for adventure and chance to see
our great WEST. Must be expert riders, willing to risk death daily.
Orphans preferred. $60 PER MONTH and keep. Apply at above address.

CHAPTER ONE

THE PONY EXPRESS: A GREAT AMERICAN ADVENTURE

A BRIEF HISTORY AND OVERVIEW

It certainly was not the first attempt at a horse-borne mail system. Post riders had operated throughout the original thirteen colonies, and as early as the first half of the thirteenth century the Mongol successors of the emperor Genghis Khan instituted a system of fast couriers to relay messages across their extensive dominions. Their network was remarkably similar to the Pony Express, with relays every thirty-five miles.

Nor was it the only horseback mail service in the American West. Several mail relay services linked California towns and mining camps in the 1850s, and a horse relay system was evidently tried between San Francisco and Oregon. During the Black Hills gold rush mail riders operated at various times between Fort Laramie, Sidney, and Deadwood, and in 1863 a service ran from Fort Bridger north to Bannack, Montana. But the well-organized (though short-lived) service between St. Joseph, Missouri, and Sacramento, California, was the run that caught the nation's imagination, the run officially known as The Pony Express, often referred to simply as "The Pony."

Before 1860 the settled part of the United States ended at about the Missouri-Kansas border. Both railroad and telegraph had met their western terminus at the river town of St. Joseph, Missouri. Beyond was a huge wilderness, nearly two thousand miles of prairie, mountain, and desert, all the way to the far side of the Sierras in the new state of California. Except for the Mormon communities in Utah and a few isolated wilderness forts, the West was untamed.

Of course there was little if any mail service. This was a matter of concern for the growing population of California. With the rush to the

Cancelled letters carried on centennial Pony Express reride, 1960 (displayed at Gilman's).

California goldfields, starting in 1848, the population of the new state grew quickly. Most of the California miners had recently arrived from the East and Midwest, and they yearned for news from back home. The folks out west just felt cut off.

The mail between California and the East had to go either by boat (with a difficult land crossing at Panama), or by a long stagecoach route through Texas and Arizona. Either way it could be a month or more for mail to get through, if it got through at all.

Huge silver strikes in Nevada and a gold rush in Colorado did much to support the need for a central overland transport and mail route. Mass emigration to the new mining districts meant more clamor for mail in the western wilderness.

In 1851 George Chorpenning was given a contract for a monthly pack mule service between Sacramento and Salt Lake, to take thirty days each way. The first trip east didn't make it on time. The first trip west didn't make it at all. In spite of such problems Chorpenning's "Jackass Mail" eventually had stations established every twenty to forty miles (many of these were later used by the stage and Pony Express).

From the east, Samuel Woodson held a government mail contract in 1850, from Independence, Missouri, to Salt Lake City. These early mail services established the basic route of the later Overland Stage and Pony Express.

CENTRAL VERSUS SOUTHERN

There was a fair amount of political wrangling over who would get the government subsidies that might make mail service profitable. There were also sectional disagreements between southern and northern politicians eager to bring western territories into their political spheres. It was understood that the mail and stage services would do much to tie the wilderness outposts to the regions served by either northern or southern rail lines, and hence align the western territories with either North or South.

In 1857 John Butterfield was given a government subsidy to provide semi-weekly coach transport of mail and passengers between St. Louis and San Francisco. The Butterfield route ran through Arkansas, Texas, and Arizona and connected with a branch route from Memphis. It clearly linked California with the South and would likely encourage the settlement of Missouri, Arkansas, and Texas, rather than Kansas Territory and the mountain regions to the north, where the Oregon and California trails (along with the Chorpenning and Woodson services) had established a viable "central route."

Supporters of both routes knew that whichever mail line won out would likely establish the course of the eventual railroad line. There was far more at stake here than a few letters from home for lonely miners in the West.

In Washington, postal officials and congressional committees (dominated by powerful Southern congressmen) were not enthusiastic about the central route. Opposition was ostensibly based on the severity of the western deserts and the unfavorable winter conditions in the Rockies and Sierras. On the other hand, the chief complaint against the southern route was that it was one thousand miles longer than the central, with even greater Indian threats in New Mexico and Arizona than from the Plains Indians to the north.

ENTER RUSSELL, MAJORS, & WADDELL

The freighting company of Russell, Majors, & Waddell was perhaps the most important transport business of the pre-Civil War West. William H. Russell was a brash visionary, a promoter, a schemer, and a gambler—a proper frontier entrepreneur. His partners, William Waddell and Alexander Majors, were conservative by comparison, but had the shrewdness and work ethic common to all successful frontier businessmen. Together they formed one of the most dynamic pioneering business partnerships in the 1850s West.

When he failed to convince his partners to start a stage line to Denver, in 1859, Russell formed an outside partnership and quickly had a lavishly-equipped line running. After three months, the new line was so heavily in debt (with the firm of Russell, Majors, & Waddell stuck with

Bronze statue of a Pony Express rider, Marysville, Kansas.

most of the notes) that Majors and Waddell were forced to take over the venture they had originally rejected.

In that same year Russell took over the government contracts of the J. M. Hockaday Company to carry mail from the Missouri River to Salt Lake City, essentially along what would eventually become the Central Overland route. Russell transferred most of the Denver stages to the Central Overland route, to Julesburg, then down to Denver or to Salt Lake via Fort Laramie and Fort Bridger.

Russell's bold schemes, put into action with the reluctant but nonetheless energetic and capable backing of his partners, were to lead the trio along a path that would ensure them an honored place in the pioneer history of the American West.

Russell, Majors, & Waddell added new stations to the ones they had inherited, well supplied with fresh mules and stock tenders, and put individual sections of the route under the supervision of their most capable men. Because of their superior organization, they lowered the coach time to Salt Lake from twenty-one days to ten days. This system of numerous and efficient relay stations was to become the foundation of the later Pony Express.

Unfortunately this highly efficient stage system, though a huge success from the traveler's standpoint, wasn't making any money. The mail contracts inherited from Hockaday were small. The owners of the new Central Overland California and Pike's Peak Express Company needed contracts and subsidies on the scale of Butterfield's. But official Washington still had its reservations, still based on the presumed impracticality of the more northerly route. What the supporters of the Central Overland route needed was a major publicity event, something that might prove, in spectacular fashion, that the central route would work regardless of the season.

In 1860 Russell, Majors, & Waddell announced plans for a fast, direct mail service between St. Joseph, Missouri, and San Francisco, California, to begin that April. Mail would be carried between these cities every week by teams of riders. The challenge was to cover this route, almost two thousand miles, in just ten days.

A MODEL OF ORGANIZATION AND EFFICIENCY

The mail was carried in four small boxes, called cantinas, attached to each corner of a flat piece of leather and designed to fit over a light saddle. This piece of leather was called a *mochila* (Spanish for knapsack). When the riders changed horses, they just pulled the mochila from the saddle and threw it onto the saddle of the fresh horse. This allowed them to change horses, and perhaps grab a quick drink of water, in less than two minutes.

Inside the boxes up to twenty pounds of letters, telegrams, and newspapers printed on tissue paper were carried in waterproofed silk pockets. At five dollars per half-ounce, weight was definitely a factor.

The organizers of this mail service already had many stagecoach stations in place. Between these stations they added smaller stations, called "swing" or "relay" stations, where the riders could change horses. At first these were placed about every twenty-five miles, but by the end of the summer of 1860 their number had increased to 190, at an average distance of ten to twelve miles. This meant that the riders could push their horses fast and change them often. At each station was a station keeper, a stock tender, and at least two fresh horses.

At regular intervals were the home stations, where the riders would pass the riding chores on to the next rider. The Express riders stayed in the home stations until the mail rider came from the other direction. Then they carried the mail back to where they originally started from. This meant that the riders and the horses covered a fairly small section of the trail (riders, about seventy-five to one hundred miles, horses, only ten or twelve miles), carrying the mail in both directions. On extremely arduous or extended rides, as in winter snows or when a rider had to immediately return with the mail from the other direction, the Express riders trusted their horses' knowledge of their section of the trail to the point that they would sometimes nap in the saddle.

The operators of this new fast mail service did not expect it to make money. They merely wanted to prove that their central route was the best way between east and west. If they could do this it might lead to rich government mail contracts.

Marker at Marysville, Kansas, showing the locations of the first stations along the route.

This would prove to be one of the most glorious chapters in the exciting history of the American frontier. It would also be a rough and dangerous experiment for the young riders and the brave men who manned the remote stations.

HOW STATIONS WERE PLACED

Several of the older stage stations were located at major forts along the route and at existing communities such as Salt Lake City, Dayton, and Carson City. But the single most important criterion was distance from the previous station. If water and timber for building were available, that was convenient, but the rule of ten to fifteen miles between stations had to be maintained, even if it meant hauling feed and water in by wagon.

Stations were generally supplied by ox train. This was another point the partners had in their favor, since freighting was their original business. The real key to the exceptional efficiency of the Pony Express was that it ran in perfect consort with Russell, Majors, & Waddell's other ventures, the Central Overland stage and their extensive freighting lines.

It is wrong to assume that one set trail was followed by every rider on every run, or that the same stations served for the entire duration of the Pony Express service.

There is reasonable evidence that there were several Pony Express rides between Sacramento and San Francisco, even though the usual procedure was to transport the mail by river steamer between these cities. There were, for those rides, relay stations along this land route.

Due to season, weather, and road conditions, the actual route appears to have changed slightly from time to time. This meant that station locations also occasionally changed—the same 190 stations did not stay constant over the entire nineteen months that the Pony Express operated. This was especially true of the western end of the line, where the advance of the railroad determined the western terminus, since there was no reason for a rider to cover ground that trains rolled easily across.

As early as July 1, 1860, Folsom rail station replaced Sacramento as the westernmost station for the riders. On earlier runs between Placerville and Sacramento, the route actually bypassed Folsom to the south, so moving the western terminus to Folsom also changed the location of the route and relay stations between Folsom and Placerville. By the end of the service the western terminus had moved eastward to Placerville.

The advance of telegraph lines also determined the locations of some stations, particularly near the close of the Pony Express. Since the riders carried telegraph messages across the ever-decreasing gap between the last telegraph stations east and west, the riders would have to drop these messages at the first telegraph station at the opposite extreme of the gap for immediate transmission ahead. This was good reason for the last telegraph station at either end of this decreasing gap to become at least a remount station.

Smaller-scale alterations of the route led to other variations in the station sequence. This helps to explain why two sites that are much too close to one another to ever have served as stations at the same time may rightfully claim to have been Pony Express stations.

Because the service ran for such a short duration, and because many of the stations were in wilderness areas that never became settled, many of the stations vanished almost as soon as the service ended. Even stations that doubled as stage stops disappeared with the end of stage travel in the West. For most of the old stations nothing remained but the dim memories of a few oldtimers, until historians began the difficult task of reconstructing the old route and locating the original stations. This task is as yet unfinished, and experts still debate and admit a certain vagueness about what was where.

Discrepancies and arguments also abound about the running of the service, about who rode where and when, about who was killed by Indians, and who made the longest and most daring rides. As with all great episodes of history, the story of the Pony Express has been caught up in legend, romance, and embellishment. Because the riders rode their way into fame and legend, there must have been more than a few oldtimers around the turn of the century collecting free drinks in western saloons on the claim—spurious or not—of having been one of that select group. And it's such a great honor for western folk to claim a Pony rider in the family tree that a great-granddaddy who simply delivered mail locally by horseback is easily transformed into one of those daring young Express riders, so that today it seems like every other person you meet in the West can claim an ancestor who rode for the Pony.

THE WEST IN 1860-1861

One might wonder why there was no Pony Express station at North Platte, Sydney, Douglas, Evanston, Austin, or so many other towns the trail passes through or near. The answer is, simply, these places didn't exist in 1860.

In fact contemporary maps reveal that remarkably few of the towns we know today existed at that time. Many of the stage and Pony Express stations were attached to isolated wilderness ranches, or were built from scratch to fit the ten- to fifteen-mile scheme. Towns did not automatically grow around the station sites. When the service ended in 1861 stations not needed as stage stops were closed. Later townsites were placed according to practical features such as water, rail lines, and pasturage rather than a set ten- to fifteen-mile plan. As a consequence today's towns are often miles distant from the old station sites.

The American West at the start of the Civil War was not the Hollywood West: cattle drives, saloon shootouts, and range wars were more typical of the West of the 1880s than of the time of the Pony Express. But the legend of the Pony Express tends to mix freely with our perception of the West of two decades later. The 1870s and 1880s saw tremendous changes in the character of the West: the completion of new railroad lines, several major mining booms, and an increase in both foreign immigration and out-migration from the defeated Confederate States. These events brought thousands of new settlers into what had once been a vast interior wilderness. By the 1880s the American West had been radically transformed from the time of the Pony Express. Most of the towns that we associate with the Wild West didn't even exist in 1860.

And yet, when we try to visualize what these trails were like for the riders, one great paradox is that even across the most remote stretches of high Wyoming plains and blank Nevada desert, places where today we can drive for fifty miles and not find a single dwelling, there were regularly-spaced express stations, every ten to fifteen miles. In this odd way some of these places are actually more remote and less inhabited now than they were in 1860-1861.

While there were few towns along the way, the trail itself was not total wilderness at all. Because of the stations, a rider was seldom more than five miles from shelter and company. And there were other travelers on the road as well. By 1860 traffic along the emigrant trails had subsided somewhat, but they still saw a steady flow westward.

In some places, the west hasn't changed much since 1860-1861. Butte Valley, Nevada, today.

Pony Express statue at St. Joseph, Missouri.

Pony Express museum, St. Joseph, Missouri.

THE YOUNG RIDERS AND THEIR SWIFT PONIES

The new mail service needed special men to do the hard work of riding long hours, in all weather, across a rough and dangerous land. It was clear from the start that not just anyone would do.

Actually, most of the riders were older than eighteen, but usually not by much. They had to be hard-working, fearless, and physically tough. And they were all screened for what the owners felt was "high moral quality." Those selected had to pledge not to drink alcohol, use profanity, or fight. But above all else, they had to prove themselves first-rate riders. Riding contests were held in the streets outside hiring centers, where the young riders competed for the prized jobs.

Riders would cover as much as four hundred miles on two runs in each direction every week. Considering the rough conditions, and the constant pressure of sticking to the schedule no matter what, it's no wonder so many riders dropped out. Though there were never more than eighty riders at any one time, nearly two hundred young men are known to have ridden for The Pony. Perhaps twenty lasted the entire nineteen months.

Yet in spite of the strict selection process and the difficulties of the job, the operators of the Pony Express never lacked for riders. The pay was good: at least fifty dollars per month, plus room and board. This may not sound like much today, but at the time it was generous—more than three times a cavalry soldier's pay.

Part of the attraction of becoming an Express rider was the thrill of danger, and the excitement of being part of this important new type of communication. To ride for the Pony was one of the greatest honors a young man could achieve. The riders had status and respect wherever they went. But the greatest attraction of being a Pony rider, more important than pay or status, was the real sense of adventure.

Just as important as the quality of the riders was the quality of the horses that carried them. The service started with three hundred specially chosen horses, bought at prices up to four times what normal horses cost. Legend has it that these horses were branded "XP," though historians have so far been unable to document this. At the height of operation five hundred of the very best horses were required for the service.

For the prairie country of the eastern part of the route, the fastest thoroughbred stock was used. In the rough desert and mountain country, west of Fort Laramie, the best native mustangs were purchased. Morgans and pintos were also favored. The Pony Express horses were prized for their toughness and endurance.

The horses were not only selected from the finest stock, but their rich diet of grains kept them so much stronger than the grass-fed Indian ponies that they could easily outrun anything that chased them. And though the horses were worked hard on the trail, they were given the

PONY EXPRESS

St. JOSEPH, MISSOURI to CALIFORNIA
in 10 days or less.

 **WANTED**

YOUNG, SKINNY, WIRY FELLOWS

not over eighteen. Must be expert riders, willing to risk death daily.

Orphans preferred.
Wages $25 per week.

APPLY, **PONY EXPRESS STABLES**
St. JOSEPH, MISSOURI

Jason Abbott, guide at Pony Express Museum, demonstrates a replica saddle/ mochila to a young visitor.

very best treatment, under strict orders from the company owners themselves. After all, the performance of these horses was counted on not only for the safe delivery of the mail but for the very lives of the young men who rode them.

Because of the fame of the Pony Express, and the youth of the riders, former Pony riders were in great demand for many exciting jobs after the service ended. They were natural choices for the dangerous position of army scout. The start of the Civil War and increased settlement of the American West provided opportunities for many of them to remain in the saddle. Many riders and station keepers found work with the new stagecoach lines and express mail companies starting up throughout the West.

A high proportion of the express riders went on to great success in later life. Several became wealthy from mining and other business ventures. Four riders from Utah later became Mormon bishops. The most famous of all the express employees was a fellow named William Cody, who went on to great fame as a scout, hunter and showman—the legendary "Buffalo Bill."

FIRST RIDE

There are several hotly-disputed claimants for the honor of having been the first to carry the mochila westward from St. Joseph. By the most convincing evidence, Johnny Fry (often variously spelled in later accounts, Frey or Frye) appears to have been the first rider, on a bay mare named Sylph. The late arrival of the train bearing the express mail from the east meant that Fry left St. Joe in twilight and well behind schedule.

The first westward ride went fairly close to schedule, with great fanfare in settlements along the way. William Hamilton, after carrying the mochila into Sacramento in the early evening of April 13, continued with his pony on the night boat to San Francisco, where he arrived just after midnight and was escorted to the Alta Telegraph Company by a throng of celebrants and a band.

The first eastbound trip of the Pony Express began from San Francisco more as a boat trip than a horse ride. James Randall galloped his horse with the mail from the offices of the Alta Telegraph Company down to the Sacramento River boat, probably more for ceremony than anything else. It is likely that the horse never even left San Francisco, as the mail proceeded to Sacramento by boat. William Hamilton rode the real first leg, from Sacramento to Sportsman's Hall, where he was re-

Pony Express motif on a wall in downtown St. Joseph (part of airline logo).

lieved by young Warren Upson, who had the daunting task of battling his way over the spine of the Sierra (in heavy spring snows), then on down to Carson City.

Between Salt Lake City and Fort Bridger the first eastbound riders were slowed by bad weather and heavy late-season snows. Once beyond South Pass they raced along in good conditions and regained their schedule. At Julesburg heavy spring runoffs had swollen the South Platte River and the rider and his mount were swept away in the swift current. The rider managed to strip the waterproofed mochila from the horse and swim to shore (his horse was reportedly rescued farther downstream), where he borrowed a fresh horse from one of the onlookers who had gathered at the river to cheer the first mail ride!

Johnny Fry covered the final sixty miles back to St. Joseph, arriving before a jubilant crowd at 3:55 on the afternoon of April 13. From St. Joe the most urgent messages were sent by telegraph, along with the news of the successful completion of the first run. Four days later the Express mail arrived in New York City by rail. Over the next nineteen months the riders covered a total of 616,000 miles, carrying 35,000 pieces of mail. Only one mochila is known to have been lost and only one rider known to have been killed in service.

THE END OF THE TRAIL

The advance of the telegraph line (from both the eastern and western ends of the Pony Express line) was inevitable and had an effect on the Pony service throughout its operation. In November of 1860, news of Abraham Lincoln's election was telegraphed from St. Louis to Fort Kearny, then was carried in just seven days to the eastern end of the western telegraph line at Fort Churchill where it went back on the wire. This indicates that the telegraph surely was creeping along from both ends.

In late October of 1861 the telegraph line connecting East and West was finally joined in Salt Lake City. This meant the end of the Pony Express, as everyone knew it would.

The Pony Express lasted only nineteen months. It lost hundreds of thousands of dollars for its owners, and the valuable mail contracts the owners were counting on were given to a competing stage company. One year after the Pony Express ended the Central Overland California and Pike's Peak Company were sold at auction. In business terms the Pony Express was certainly not a success.

But the Pony could hardly be called a failure. It proved once and for all the practicality of the Central Overland route. This same route was slightly altered a few years later for the transcontinental railroad line.

Perhaps the most significant contribution of the Pony was how it linked California and the Utah and Kansas territories to the Union at the

Pony Express statue, Old Sacramento.

start of the Civil War. The mail connection with the East, during the critical period of 1860 and 1861, was very important in keeping these rich and productive lands in the Union.

Today the image of the solitary Pony rider, like the lonely prospector, the cowboy, the Indian warrior, and the cavalry soldier, is one of the most important symbols of the West, a personification of the tremendous spirit and daring that forged a great empire from the high prairie, rugged mountains, and forbidding deserts. The riders of the Pony Express helped tie together the unsettled wilderness and connect it to the rest of the nation. For this great service their story lives on in the legends of the American West.

Pony Express bronze at Marysville, Kansas.

CHAPTER TWO

HOW TO USE THIS GUIDE

ORGANIZATION

The original route of the Pony Express ran both east-west and west-east, and there are equally strong arguments for organizing this guide to run in either direction. In choosing to organize this as an east-west guide, I adhere to a fairly traditional prejudice of viewing movement in the American West as primarily a west-progressing affair. To travelers for whom an eastward progression is more convenient, I can only beg indulgence, and offer the suggestion that perhaps a quick jaunt east, then a slow drive westward might be in order.

This guide is broken down into five individual geographic regions, rather than state by state. I have long viewed the American West as actually several distinct Wests, and the route of the Pony Express can truly be seen as traversing several disparate regions that are not necessarily defined by state boundaries.

As the modern traveler moves westward, it becomes clear that points of interest relate more and more to the landscape than to historical events or man-made attractions. In general, things to see along the Missouri/Kansas/Nebraska portion of the trail are historical and people-oriented, while the Wyoming/Utah/Nevada regions are most remarkable for their rugged mountain scenery and glorious desert vistas.

This is not meant to be a mile-by-mile guide to the exact route of the Pony Express, nor will this book lead you to the exact sites of all 190 (possibly more) of the original stations, most of which disappeared long ago. This is a general driving guide to the regions through which the Pony Express passed, with specific references to significant sites of interest to Pony Express enthusiasts, as well as to a variety of non-Pony attractions.

I have highlighted several "Pony Express Byway" drives, which are essentially off-the-beaten-track mini tours along the old trail. Some of these involve variations depending on the suitability of individual vehicles for roads of varying roughness.

Note that the official road maps to each of the states through which the old trail passed do indicate the approximate route of the Pony Express. This may sometimes be useful for seeing more clearly where the trail passed in relation to present roads and towns. By all means, use this guide in conjunction with the road maps. While not entirely necessary, some travelers might want to purchase more detailed topographical maps (especially useful are the maps of the South Pass, Wyoming, area and certain desert areas of western Utah and Nevada). These are available at Bureau of Land Management (BLM) offices in most major towns enroute.

For each community mentioned along the route, this guide book indicates what services are available. At the end of each entry for substantial communities, there is also an address and/or phone number for local travel information.

SAMPLE ITINERARIES

You could conceivably do a reasonable eight-day gallop of the old Pony route, although you certainly would not have time to poke around or do the more time-consuming Pony Byways. It might run something like this:

Day One: St. Joseph, Missouri, to Rock Creek/Fairbury, Nebraska; about 140 miles.
U.S. Highway 36 across northeastern Kansas to Marysville. North on US 77, then west on Nebraska Highway 8 to Fairbury.

Day Two: Fairbury to Bridgeport, Nebraska; 420 to 450 miles, depending on route chosen.
Follow route of individual choice to Kearny. Then Interstate 80 or US 30 west to Brule. West on I-80/76 to Julesburg, Colorado. North on US 385 to I-80, then west on I-80 to Sidney, Nebraska. North on US 385 to Bridgeport.

Day Three: Bridgeport to Casper, Wyoming; about 210 miles.
US 26 to Scottsbluff, then on to Torrington and Fort Laramie, Wyoming, and I-25. North on I-25 to Casper.

Day Four: Casper to Evanston, Wyoming; about 370 miles.
Southwest on Wyoming 220 to Muddy Gap. North and west on US 287 to Wyoming 28. South and west on Wyoming 28, through Farson, to Wyoming 372 at Seedskadee National Wildlife Refuge. South on Wyoming 372 to I-80, then west to Evanston.

Day Five: Evanston to Salt Lake City, Utah; about 81 miles.
West on I-80 to Salt Lake City.

Day Six: Salt Lake to Ely, Nevada; about 320 miles.
Fastest route: South on I-15 to US 6. South on US 6 to junction with US 50 at Delta. West on US 50/6 to Ely.
A longer day: South on I-15 to Lehi. West on Utah 73 through Fairfield, then follow desert drive through Ibapah to Schellbourne, Nevada. South on US 93 to Ely.

Day Seven: Ely to Carson City, Nevada; about 320 miles.
West on US 50 to Carson City.

Day Eight: Carson City to Sacramento, California; about 130 miles.
West on US 50 through South Lake Tahoe and Placerville to Sacramento.

Taking an extra two days would slow the pace to a more reasonable canter, and twelve days would allow for a leisurely trot.

RELATIONSHIP TO OREGON-CALIFORNIA AND MORMON TRAILS

The Pony Express route was nearly identical to the well-traveled Oregon Trail as far as western Wyoming. From Fort Bridger westward, the Pony riders followed fairly closely the trail established by the earlier Mormon pioneers and California gold hunters. Because the Pony left little physical evidence of its short but lively career, today's Pony Express enthusiasts might feel in the shadow of these important emigrant trails (and especially the celebrated Oregon Trail), in terms of markers and points of interest. This guide describes the route largely in terms of sites, attractions, and incidents of special relevance to the Pony Express.

LITERATURE OF SPECIAL RELEVANCE TO PONY EXPRESS TOURISM

There is a wealth of historic writing about the Pony Express and its riders. Among the dozens of books on the Pony, these are some of the standard works:

General historic overview:

Pony Express by Fred Reinfeld.
Saddles & Spurs: The Pony Express Saga by Raymond and Mary Settle.
Pony Express: The Great Gamble by Roy Bloss (out of print and hard to find, but has some very nice pictures of old stations).

Historic trail markers at Big Mountain Pass, east of Salt Lake City.

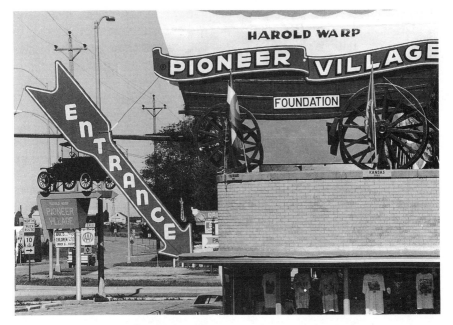

Pioneer Village, Minden, Nebraska.

For Young Readers:

The Pony Express, Hoofbeats in the Wilderness by Joseph DiCerto.
Pony Bob's Daring Ride: A Pony Express Adventure, by Joe Bensen.

Perhaps the most informative and intriguing historic description of the region, as well as the route and stations, is the account by Sir Richard Burton of his 1860 journey on the Overland Stage in The City of the Saints, and across the Rocky Mountains to California. Burton made his trip shortly after the start of the Express service, and since the stagecoach route and stations were essentially the same as for the Pony Express (and because Burton was a writer of extraordinary talent and perception), his account is generally held as the definitive contemporary description of conditions along the trail. The book is engagingly written in the finest Victorian style, and filled with the fascinating insights of this most remarkable gentleman traveler.

THE NATIONAL PONY EXPRESS ASSOCIATION

The National Pony Express Association (NPEA) is a non-profit organization devoted to keeping the spirit and legend of the Pony Express alive through group activities such as rerides of both the entire route and of shorter sections. NPEA also publishes a monthly newsletter, chock full of historical material and information on current events of interest to Pony Express fans. Write NPEA at Box 236, Pollock Pines, CA 95726, for membership information.

NATIONAL HISTORIC TRAIL STATUS

In 1992 President George Bush signed into law an act designating the Pony Express and California trails as National Historic trails. Over the next few years plans are to better mark the old trail, and several new interpretive sites will be built.

For now, however, trail markers are sporadic and interpretive sites sadly lacking. There is also the problem of "souvenir hunters" (a.k.a. vandals) physically removing Pony Express Trail markers—especially in remote desert regions of Utah and Nevada—just where travelers need them most. TAKE THIS AS A WARNING, that even where this guide refers to trail markers, these markers may not be in place.

VEHICULAR ADVICE

Have your vehicle thoroughly serviced before leaving home. This is especially true if you drive a foreign car. Attitudes toward foreign ve-

Near Austin, Nevada.

Slick dirt road, north of Deshler, Nebraska.

hicles among mechanics in this part of the world generally run from polite indifference to out-and-out automotive xenophobia. This won't be quite as big a problem from Utah westward, but just try to find that Mazda timing belt in smalltown Nebraska!

For travelers who look forward to following the actual Pony route via the rougher desert drives described in this book (especially in Nevada), I strongly suggest carrying two spare tires. Much of the desert driving in Utah and Nevada is miles from anywhere, so a single flat will send you nervously seeking the nearest town—which may be a long way out of your way. You should also take very seriously the warnings in this guide about road conditions. Not all of the alternate routes described in this book are appropriate for conventional cars and, especially, for recreational vehicles (RVs). If in doubt, it is always best to inquire locally about present road conditions.

Of course you should carry plenty of water, and always keep an eye on your gas gauge (remember that some of the rougher drives described in this book will be much harder on gas consumption than blacktop driving). Finally, if your vehicle isn't air-conditioned, a couple of large white towels are extremely useful for keeping the sun and dust off camera bags, coolers, small children, etc.

Pony Express motif of a St. Joseph motel.

NOTES ON CAMPGROUNDS, MOTELS, AND RESTAURANTS

This is not an accommodations and dining guide. Most of the reasonably large towns along the route have an adequate selection of places to eat and sleep. Where I have found an especially attractive or interesting place to eat or sleep, and in places where facilities are sparse, I point this out. Otherwise, the choice is up to personal preference.

For those depending on motel accommodations during the height of the summer tourist season, it is sometimes a good idea to reserve a room in advance even though this may put restrictions on your daily progress. Driving into Kearney or Casper or Salt Lake after dark without a room reservation shouldn't present any problems; but if you roll into a place like Farson, Wyoming, or Ibapah, Utah, at 8 p.m. looking for a room, you will likely end up driving miles out of your way in the dark before you get to sleep.

ECOLOGY AND GOOD MANNERS

Historic ruins along the Pony Express trail are cultural sites protected by federal law. Please do not damage sites or remove materials.

Much of the old trail and many of the old station sites are now on private property. It is hoped that in the future more of these sites will be accessible to the public; the BLM often negotiates land trades with owners to acquire sites of cultural or recreational importance. For the moment, our ability to visit sites on private property is entirely up to individual owners, so we must all show respect for property and try our best not to make enemies of these folks. Please remember that your actions may affect the privileges of later visitors. Don't litter, don't take "souvenirs," don't enter private property without permission, and (especially where livestock graze) shut the darned gate when you leave!

PHONE NUMBERS FOR ADDITIONAL TRAVEL INFORMATION:

Kansas Travel and Tourism Division: (913) 296-2009
Nebraska Travel and Tourism: 1 800 228-4307
Wyoming Division of Tourism: 1 800 225-5996 or (307) 777-7777
Utah Travel Council: (801) 538-1030
Nevada Commission on Tourism: 1 800 NEVADA-8
California Office of Tourism: 1 800 862-2543

LET US KNOW WHAT YOU FIND ALONG THE WAY

As interest in the history of the Pony Express builds, new interpretive sites and other Pony-related attractions may be developed. Please keep us posted on recent additions, as well as any errors or serious omissions you might discover, so we can update future editions of this guide. Write care of Falcon Press, P.O. Box 1718, Helena, MT 59624.

Finally, don't forget to stop and smell the sagebrush!

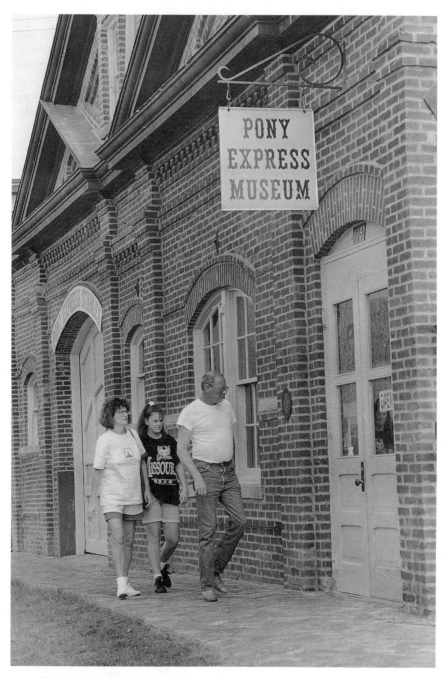

Pony Express Museum, St. Joseph.

CHAPTER THREE

THE PIONEER PRAIRIE: ST. JOSEPH, MISSOURI, TO OGALLALA, NEBRASKA

Beyond Walnut Creek a dense nimbus, rising ghostlike from the northern horizon, furnished us with a spectacle of those perilous prairie storms which make the prudent lay aside their revolvers and disembarrass themselves of their cartridges. Gusts of raw, cold, and violent wind from the west whizzed overhead, thunder crashed and rattled closer and closer, and vivid lightning, flashing out of the murky depths around, made earth and air one blaze of living fire.

—Burton, p.25

ST. JOSEPH
(all services)

St. Joseph, Missouri, was where the telegraph and the railroad from the east met the Pony Express to the west. Actually, residents of Leavenworth, Kansas, had hoped their town would be the eastern terminus for the Pony, but St. Joseph boosters offered the organizers free land and facilities for the venture.

The town has an interesting and illustrious frontier history, dating back to the successful mercantile ventures established here by pioneer merchant, Joseph Robidoux, for early traders, trappers, and emigrants to the western territories. When Robidoux laid out the original townsite, he named a street for each member of his family: his wife, Angelique; his daughter, Sylvanie; and his sons, Francis, Jules, Edmond, Charles, and Felix.

Modern "St. Joe" is a pleasant community that wears its history proudly (as a fitting touch, the St. Joseph bus system is named EXPRESS, and has a Pony Express rider for its logo). The town abounds in Victorian architecture and sites of historical interest relating to the Pony and to other aspects of the Pioneer West.

There's plenty to see here, so count on at least a day. If your schedule permits, try to tour the town on a Sunday, when it is most peaceful and traffic free. And do drive around the old center of town a bit, just to admire the many attractive old buildings.

A good starting place is the **Pony Express National Memorial** at 914 Penn Street (phone: (816) 279-5059). The museum is housed in the original Pony Express stables, where the first westbound rider (Johnny Fry) departed on April 13, 1860. Fry rode from here to the U.S. Post Office at Third and Felix streets where he picked up the mail and galloped off into history (actually, he galloped off into Kansas Territory, but it was quite the historical event nonetheless).

This museum is an absolute must-see, and an essential first orientation for anyone interested in the Pony. The exhibits are informative and entertaining, demonstrating the careful research and authenticity of professional curating. Museum volunteers are on hand to answer questions, and there is an excellent souvenir shop. Hours vary depending on season, as follows:

April through September: Monday through Saturday, 9 a.m. to 6 p.m.; Sunday, 1 p.m. to 6 p.m.
October through March: Monday through Saturday, 9 a.m. to 5 p.m.; Sunday, 1 p.m. to 5 p.m.
Closed Thanksgiving Day, December 24, 25, 31, and January 1.

Other St. Joseph Museums:

The **St. Joseph Museum** at 11th and Charles fills a beautiful Gothic mansion, overlooking the town and river. The museum holds extensive displays of the social and natural history of the region.

The **Patee House Museum** at 12th and Penn was the original St. Joseph headquarters of the Pony Express, and also the best hotel in town. It specializes in Western art and artifacts.

As an aside, check out the **Glore Psychiatric Museum** at 3400 Frederick. It has nothing to do with the Pony, but it's interesting nonetheless. Displays include treatment and restraining devices, equipment, and hospital furniture from 400 years of psychiatry.

The **Military Heritage Museum** at 701 Messanie has displays of all branches of the military, from Civil War to present.

Other St. Joseph attractions:

Pony Express Statue. 10th and Francis.

Jesse James Home. 12th and Penn. Where Bob Ford shot and killed the famous outlaw.

Robidoux Row. 3rd and Poulin. Series of connected restored houses built in 1840s by Joseph Robidoux, the founder of St. Joseph.

Tourist Information Center: Exit 47 (Frederick St.) of I-29. Holiday Inn Downtown Conference Center: 102 S. Third St. (Felix & Edmond Sts. exit of I-229).

ST. JOSEPH TO MARYSVILLE

From St. Joseph, the riders crossed the Missouri River by ferry to start the ride across northeastern Kansas. There is a plaque in Riverfront Park on the St. Joe side of the Missouri, commemorating the site of the old ferry (ask directions at the Pony Express National Memorial).

Leave St. Joseph on U.S. Highway 36 (divided highway), across the Missouri River into Kansas. US 36 quickly becomes the two-lane "Pony Express Highway."

About fifteen miles from St. Joseph is the site of the first Kansas relay station, in Troy. The original relay station was probably a few blocks to the east of the monument that stands in the northeastern corner of the courthouse square. Also on the square, note Troy's Romanesque courthouse, and the **Kansas Indian Monument** (carved from a single oak log, sixty-seven inches in diameter and twenty-seven feet high).

From Troy, the actual Pony Express route ran somewhat south and west, approximately the route of Kansas Highway 20. This region is mostly private farmland, with no real trace of the Pony beyond the odd marker for old relay stations. Unless you're adamant about tracing the original route, it is far more expedient to stick to US 36.

Twelve miles west of Troy on US 36, at Kansas 120 (and the town of Highland), turn north to the **Iowa Sac and Fox Indian Mission Museum,** an interesting non-Pony diversion if you have the time. The mission dates from 1837 and is currently undergoing major renovation. The mission will be closed until the work is completed. It is scheduled to reopen in November 1995. In the past, hours were from 10 a.m. to 5 p.m. Tuesday through Saturday; 1 p.m. to 5 p.m. Sunday; closed Monday. Admission was free; call ahead for current information.

Another fifteen miles west, in the cemetery in Hiawatha, is an odd collection of funerary sculpture known as the Davis Memorial. Just ask anyone in this small town, or follow the signs.

From Hiawatha, to make a sidetrip to the site of the old Kennekuk station, take US 159 south to Horton (thirteen miles), then continue 0.75 mile south from Horton to an improved gravel road on the left, marked "Atchison County Lake." Follow this road 1.6 miles to the Express marker and granite-block monument. The station itself stood on what is now private property. In 1860 Kennekuk had two hotels, a blacksmith and livery stable, two general stores, a post office, two churches, and about 100 residents. There really isn't much to see here today, except for some scenic farmland and pleasant old villages along the way.

Twenty-seven miles west of Hiawatha on US 36, in the town of Seneca, is the site of what might have been the first home station on the westward ride. A large stone monument marks the site at the corner of Main and Fourth. Just 0.5 mile west of Seneca is the commercial roadside attraction called **Fort Markley,** a sort of ersatz, false-front frontier town that might be of interest to younger travelers.

From Seneca, the original Pony route ran parallel to and slightly to the north of US 36. It is easy to imagine the Express riders covering this flat ground quickly.

For a good view of the sort of terrain the riders covered, take the turnoff north to Axtell (about ten miles west of Seneca), then continue north through this small town on Fifth Street to the public school on the right, at the north edge of town. Continue north on Fifth Street (it becomes a surfaced county road) 0.65 mile to the first road on the right (improved gravel). Turn right, cross the small bridge, and drive two miles to the first road on the left. Turn left and drive 0.65 mile to a prominent marker on the right (just past a red house) for Ash Point Station. The station, part of a vanished town of some thirty residents, sat 0.75 mile to the east.

Another stone marker for another vanished station can be seen just north of the town of Beattie, which is one mile north of US 36, twelve miles west of Axtell. From the black water tank marked "City of Beattie" at the west end of Elm Street, drive north on the surfaced county road 3.3 miles to the monument for Guittard's Station, on the right or east side of the road.

MARYSVILLE

(most services: garage, good selection of motels, and free RV hookups at City Park)

Marysville was established by emigrants from South Carolina, who named the place Palmetto City after the tree that graces their home state's seal. When Burton visited here, he described it as "a town which thrived by selling whiskey to ruffians of all descriptions." It is a much gentler place today.

Marysville's must-see attraction, the restored **Pony Express Barn Museum,** is found at 108 South Eighth Street. In addition to various Pony Express memorabilia (some gathered from nearby relay stations) and a replica mochila, there's an eclectic assortment of historic bric-a-brac that includes World War II Japanese military items, a complete set of 1908-1967 Kansas license plates, barbed-wire and tool collections, and a set of dolls representing Kansas's first ladies from 1869-1955. All in all,

Marysville Station.

a pretty good collection of neat old stuff. The museum also maintains an extensive research collection of books, photographs, and other material on the Pony Express. Hours are 9 a.m. to 5 p.m. daily, May 1 through September 30. Admission is $1 adults, $0.50 kids. Pony Express Barn, 106 S. 8th St.

Marysville also has a nice local museum, The Koester House Museum, and a fine old courthouse. This attractive Romanesque building at 1209 Broadway now holds a history library and exhibits of old photos and newspaper equipment. Admission is free.

MARYSVILLE TO FORT KEARNY

Just west of Marysville on US 36 (on the left or south side of the road) is a larger-than-life bronze sculpture of a Pony Express rider, along with a couple of memorial plaques.

West of Marysville, settlement became increasingly scarce as the arable prairie farmland gradually gave way to the rocky plains. About eight miles northwest of Marysville, the Pony Express Trail joined the main branch of the Oregon-California Trail, from Independence. From this point all the way to Fort Bridger, the two trails were nearly identical.

US 36 across the northeast corner of Kansas is called the "Pony Express Highway."

HOLLENBERG STATION

This important State Historic Site is fourteen miles north and west of Marysville. About ten miles west of Marysville, watch for the prominent sign for Hanover/Hollenberg Station, at Kansas 148. Note that the station is near Hanover, and not at the nearby town of Hollenberg. Just follow the conspicuous signs.

Hollenberg, on Cottonwood Creek, was established as a ranch and general store around 1858 by Gerat Hollenberg, a German immigrant who had prospected for gold in California, Australia, and Peru. Hollenberg had a thriving business, due to his ranch's strategic location on one of the most heavily traveled roads in the West. This was a popular camping place for travelers on the Oregon-California trail, and was an obvious choice for a stage station on the Central Overland route.

The old station has been faithfully maintained in its original condition, and is administered as a museum by the Kansas State Historical Society. Most of the downstairs was the private residence of the Hollenberg family, with one room serving as post office and general store, and another as a tavern. Six employees of the Overland Stage and Pony Express shared the upstairs. The site has picnic grounds with water and toilets. Hollenberg is a very popular place for weekend reenactments and other special events. Since many of these are impromptu, it may be worth call-

Pony Express reenactment at Hollenberg Station, Kansas.

ing ahead to see if anything special is going on. Phone (913) 337-2635. The station is open Tuesday through Saturday, 10 a.m. to 5 p.m.; Sunday 1 p.m. to 5 p.m.. Admission is free.

Continue north on Kansas 148 to the Kansas-Nebraska line, where a monument marks the point where the Pony Express Trail and Oregon-California Trail crossed what would later be the state line.

After a couple of twists and turns, Kansas 148 intersects Nebraska 8 at Odell. Turn left (west) and continue seventeen miles to Endicott. Just before entering town, a sign indicates the way to Rock Creek Station, about 3.5 miles north and east.

NEBRASKA TRAVEL INFORMATION

Nebraska offers a one-year parks sticker (available at all state historic/recreation sites and many convenience stores) for $10. The sticker gives entry to a variety of sites and recreational areas, including many attractive but basic camping areas that are otherwise free (most of the more elaborate state parks charge a small camping fee in addition to the entry fee). A daily parks sticker is $2, so a combination of five assorted site/park/campground visits might warrant buying the yearly sticker. Three state historical sites pertain in one way or another to the Pony Express: Rock Creek, Fort Kearny, and Buffalo Bill's Scouts' Rest Ranch.

FACTS ABOUT NEBRASKA:

1) There Is Such A Thing As Running Water And Indoor Toilets.

2) There Is Electricity And Even Televisions.

3) The State Tree Is _Not_ the Telephone Pole.

4) The Pony Express No Longer Delivers The Mail.

5) The "Long" Drive Accross The State Is What You Make Of It.

ROCK CREEK STATION

This State Historical Park features reconstructed ranch buildings and a post office, along with some prominent Oregon Trail wagon ruts. There are camping and picnic facilities. Visitor center hours are 9 a.m. to 5 p.m. daily in summer, 1 p.m. to 5 p.m. weekends in May, September, and October. A daily or annual parks permit is required.

Wild Bill at Rock Creek

Rock Creek was the site of one of the most dramatic (and certainly one of the most sordid) events in Pony Express history. In July of 1861, a twenty-three-year-old stable hand from Illinois named Jim Hickok shot David McCanles and two other unarmed men, launching a career and starting a legend second only to Buffalo Bill Cody's in the history of the American West.

David McCanles had come here from North Carolina in the Pike's Peak gold rush of 1859. He lost his gold fever along the way, saw the business potential of the Rock Creek stream crossing, and purchased the primitive stage station and store established here two years earlier. McCanles built a toll bridge and a small building for lease to the Central Overland Company, which kept its own employees here.

A strong animosity arose between McCanles and Central Overland employee Hickok, perhaps based on sectional differences relating to the Civil War. The bad blood was no doubt aggravated by McCanles's habit of calling Hickok "Duck Bill," in reference to the latter's prominent nose and upper lip.

Rock Creek Station State Park.

Rock Creek Post Office, 1865.

When McCanles confronted the Central Overland's station keeper, Horace Wellman, about overdue payments, Hickok interceded on behalf of his boss, killing the unarmed McCanles and wounding McCanles's help.

Whether it was Hickok who "finished off" the other two men was never determined; nor has it ever been decided whether it was an act of self defense or cold-blooded murder. At the trial, the only testimony heard was from the defendants and from Wellman's wife, and the incident was ruled self defense. McCanles's twelve-year-old son Monroe, an eye-witness to the killings, was not allowed to testify, due to his age. Many years later, as a respected Kansas City attorney, Monroe McCanles gave a sworn statement that completely contradicted the Hickok/Wellman version.

These were the shady circumstances that inaugurated the dramatic career of one of the West's most celebrated gunfighters. Of course, by the time the dime-novel writers were finished embellishing the tale, "Wild Bill" had single-handedly defeated all ten members of the vicious "M'Kandlas gang," shrugging off his own thirteen wounds. Bill's career ended fifteen years later in a Deadwood saloon, shot in the back while holding a pair of aces and a pair of eights.

There isn't much of real interest concerning the Pony Express between Rock Creek and Kearney, except for a handful of markers for vanished stations. Sticking fairly close to the Oregon Trail, the riders fol-

MAP 1: MARYSVILLE, KS, TO KEARNEY, NE

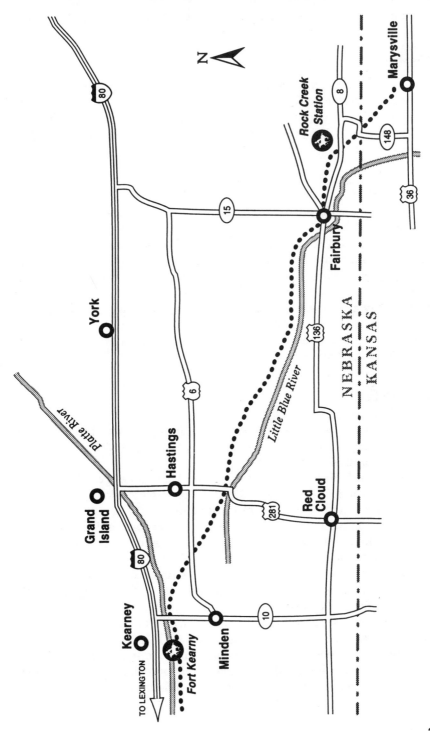

lowed the Little Blue River, which today cuts across field and farmland at a distance from any main roads. How you choose to drive from Rock Creek to Kearney will probably depend on which of the following (non-Pony) attractions most appeal to you.

Sidetrips in South-Central Nebraska

Try to visit either Pioneer Village in Minden, or Stuhr's Museum of the Prairie Pioneer in Grand Island. These are both "attraction intensive sites," with TONS of great things to see, but only the most avid sightseer will need to see both. Visiting both on consecutive days might produce tourist overload.

RED CLOUD

Red Cloud is the site of the **Willa Cather Historical Center.** Operated by the Nebraska State Historical Society, this museum houses the Cather Archives. The nearby art gallery and book store carries the most complete collection of works by and about this important American writer. Five miles south of town is the **Cather Memorial Prairie,** more than 600 acres of native grassland. Tours of Cather's childhood home are offered daily at 9:30 a.m., 11 a.m., 1:30 p.m., 2:45 p.m., and 4 p.m. Museum hours are 8 a.m. to 12 noon and 1 p.m. to 5 p.m., Monday through Friday; 1 p.m. to 5 p.m., Saturday and Sunday (closed Monday from October 1 through April 30).

HASTINGS

(all services)

Hastings is a small town with an astounding variety of attractions, featuring everything from the birthplace of KOOL-AID (invented here in 1927) to Micronesian cultural artifacts.

If you enter Hastings from the east on US 6, note the miles of huge bunkers on the left. Here, on 35,000 acres of Nebraska farmland, the U.S. Navy planted its largest munitions depot. Today, the old depot serves as an industrial park, housing more than forty industries. If you wish, you may drive around the complex of bunkers, which extends for miles out onto the prairie.

Hastings's most popular attraction is its fine museum at 1330 North Burlington Avenue (corner of US 281 and 14th St.), housing one of the Midwest's best collections of natural and pioneer history. Among the many displays is one highlighting Edwin Perkins's invention of America's favorite powdered drink mix. An IMAX theater opened in June, 1994. Also located in the Hastings Museum is the J.M. McDonald Planetarium, offering public sky shows seven days a week. Museum hours are 9 a.m. to 5 p.m. Monday through Saturday; 1 p.m. to 5 p.m.

Sunday and holidays (closed New Year's, Thanksgiving, and Christmas Day). Planetarium shows are given Memorial Day through Labor Day: Monday through Saturday 11 a.m., 1:30 p.m., 3:30 p.m.; Sunday 2:30 p.m., 3:30 p.m. Rest of year: daily 2:30 p.m., 3:30 p.m. plus an 11 a.m. Saturday show. Admission is $4 for adults, $3.50 for seniors, $2 for ages 6-15, under 6 free.

Native artifacts from New Guinea? In Nebraska? Hey, no problem. The American Crosier Brothers have been ministering to the Asmat people of Irian Jaya (on the island of New Guinea) since 1958, encouraging them to preserve and develop their unique crafts. **The Crosier Asmat Museum** is located on the grounds of the Crosier Monastery, on 13th Street, eight blocks east of the Hastings Museum. The collection consists mostly of wood carvings (including fifteen-foot ancestor poles), along with shields, spirit masks, drums with lizard-skin drumheads, boar-tusk bracelets, and human jawbone necklaces. No real hours, but please call ahead to arrange a tour: (402) 463-3188. Donations are accepted.

Hastings also features nightly computerized water and light shows at Fisher Fountain (Highland Park, 12th and Denver Sts.), from mid-May to September. For other attractions in and around Hastings, call the Adams County Visitors Bureau at 1 800 967-2189.

CLAY CENTER

Red meat? In Nebraska? You better believe it! Rather less of a surprise than jawbone necklaces from New Guinea is the **U.S. Meat Animal Research Center,** three miles west of Clay Center. Here, at the largest facility of its kind in the world, scientists study 12,000 cattle, sheep, and hogs to develop new ways of increasing production of high-quality red meats. The public (including vegetarians) are welcome. Hours are 8 a.m. to 4:30 p.m., Monday through Friday. To arrange for a (free) guided tour, call ahead: (402) 762-3241.

GRAND ISLAND

(all services)

Grand Island is the home of the **Stuhr Museum of the Prairie Pioneer.** This immense (200-acre) complex tells the story of prairie settlement, complete with a recreated 1860s railroad town (with sixty individual buildings), a relocated ranch, and a full-sized reconstruction of a Pawnee earth lodge. There are extensive displays of old farm machinery, period home furnishings, and Native American memorabilia, and a fascinating seven-acre railyard exhibit.

This is one of the better historical interpretation museums in the country. Plan on a minimum of three hours here. Indoor exhibits and displays are open year-round. The railroad town, railyard exhibit, farm

Approximate route of the Pony Express, Adams County, Nebraska.

machinery and auto exhibits, and restored communities are open May 1 through October 15. Hours are 9 a.m. to 5 p.m. every day (1 p.m. to 5 p.m. on Sunday, from October 16 through April 30) Admission from May 1 through October 15: Adults $6; Seniors $5.50; Ages 7-16 $3.50; Under 7 free. From October 16 through April 30: Adults $4; Seniors $3.50; Ages 7-16 $2; Under 7 free.

MINDEN

(most services)

Harold Warp's Pioneer Village is perhaps the most interesting commercial tourist attraction in the entire Midwest, with more than 50,000 historical items, organized (more or less) on the theme of progress. In twenty-eight jam-packed buildings, you'll find much to enthuse over, *including* the kitchen sink. There's a sod house, a one-room schoolhouse, a replica of a Pony Express station, farm machinery, bicycle and auto displays, and much, much more.

While it may lack the accuracy of professionally curated collections, this place is not only worth seeing, but a real treasure trove on the tourist trail. This is the grand-scale version of all those hodge-podge county historical society museums whose greatest attraction is in the accumulation of lots of neat old stuff. The remarkable thing about Pioneer Village is that this terrific eclectic jumble was assembled by one man, Mr. Harold Warp. A restaurant, motel, and campground are on the grounds (and all

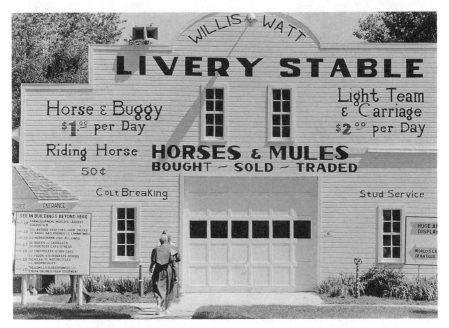

Pioneer Village in Minden, Nebraska.

services are available in town). The price of admission ($5 for adults, $2.50 for kids, under 6 free) is good for as many consecutive days as you care to poke around, and the Village is open daily, 8 a.m. to sundown. Call 1 800 445-4447 for more information.

KEARNEY

(all services)

Yes, that's right, the name of the town and the old fort are spelled differently. Evidently, an extra e was added by someone at the post office many years ago and no one ever bothered to correct the spelling. The present town of Kearney is on the northern bank of the Platte River, while the Pony Express and Oregon-California Trail ran along the southern bank.

FORT KEARNY STATE HISTORICAL PARK AND RECREATIONAL AREA

Fort Kearny was the first and easternmost of six military forts built to protect the pre-Civil War expansion of white interests in the West. During an eighteen-month period in 1848-1849, some 30,000 people passed through Fort Kearny on their way to Oregon, the California goldfields, and the Mormon enclave of Salt Lake City.

Tad Casper, giving a blacksmith demonstration at the Fort Kearny State Historical Park.

In 1860-1861 this was, in many ways, the edge of the western frontier. From here, cavalry patrols provided protection for Oregon Trail emigrants, for isolated farms and ranches, and for the stage and Pony Express as well.

It is questionable whether a Pony Express station ever existed at the military post itself. The actual Kearny Express Station was a home station located at a place called Dogtown (and long disappeared), which was just to the northeast of the town of Lowell, about seven miles east of the fort. The next station was at Dobytown, two miles west of the fort, denoted today by a prominent marker.

The fort's last important function was providing protection for the work crews building the Union Pacific Railroad. The military abandoned the fort in 1871 when troubles with the Indians appeared to be over, and its buildings were gradually removed.

The present forty-acre park is located six miles southeast of the town of Kearney. Cross the Platte either from town, or take the next Interstate 80 exit east of Kearney (exit 279). Either way is well marked. The park has an interpretive center, along with a working blacksmith-carpenter shop, and a replica of the 1864 stockade (built during the serious Indian uprisings of that year and well after the demise of the Pony Express). Grounds are open year-round from 8 a.m. to 8 p.m. The interpretive center is open daily from 9 a.m. to 5 p.m. in the summer, and from 1 p.m. to 5 p.m. on weekends in May, September, and October. A Nebraska park permit ($2/day, $10/year) is required.

Just 0.75 mile east and one mile north of the historical park is **Fort Kearny State Recreation Area**, offering hiking trails, swimming, fishing, boating, and a really first-rate campground with showers and electrical hookups. A camping fee is charged in addition to the $2 park permit, but the park permit also gains admission at the historical park on same day.

Half a million **Sandhill cranes** show up on the Platte during late March and early April. The bridge on Nebraska 10 south of Kearney provides an ideal spot for crane watching; sunset and sunrise are the best times. While the cranes are in residence, daily lectures on cranes and a crane-watching film are regularly offered at Fort Kearny.

Other things to see in Kearney:

Museum of Nebraska Art. 24th and Central. Art work by Nebraskans or about Nebraska. Closed Mondays and major holidays. Free.

Trails and Rails Museum. 710 west 11th St. Restored buildings, railroad exhibits. Daily, Memorial Day to Labor Day. Free. For more Kearny-area visitor information call: 1 800 652-9435 in-state; 1 800 227-8340 nationally

From the point just east of Fort Kearny where the trail encountered the Platte River, to just east of Julesburg, the express route (as well as the main branch of the emigrant trails) followed the Platte along its southern bank. At Julesburg, the riders forded the South Platte River, then struck north to rejoin the south bank of the North Branch of the Platte, which it followed as far as the old toll bridge at the present site of Casper, Wyoming.

East of Fort Kearny, the Pony Express trail ran through well-settled country, along well-traveled roads. But between Fort Kearny and the Sierra Nevada lay a vast, rough wilderness. Not that the trail itself was especially hard to follow. Twenty years of steady emigrant travel along the Platte River and across the Wyoming plains had etched the trail so clearly into the earth that the track can still be seen today in many places. But even the relatively fertile valley of the Platte was sparsely populated compared to the Kansas prairie, and except for isolated settlements at Julesburg and Fort Laramie, there wasn't much more than the occasional wilderness ranch, many of which served as stage and express stations.

COZAD
(most services)

Willow Island Station, originally about nine miles southeast of Cozad, was moved to the town park back in the 1930s. Artist Robert Henri, founder of the American Ash Can School, grew up here, and the Henri home is now a museum.

GOTHENBURG
(most services)

Gothenburg calls itself "The Pony Express Capital of Nebraska" and the Pony emblem is seen in abundance around town. Here is a good opportunity to see another transplanted station, as well as one on its original site. **Gilman's Station** was moved to Ehman Park in 1931 from its original site four miles west of Fort McPherson, as a gift from the Williams family. Today it serves as a tourist attraction and information office, and has the best selection of Pony-related souvenirs west of St. Joseph. Just follow the numerous signs to Ehman Park.

Three miles south of Gothenburg is one of the best examples of an original Pony Express station still on its original site. Drive south from town on Nebraska 47 to the Lower 96 Ranch, where the owners (the same family who presented Gilman's Station to the city of Gothenburg) have been extremely gracious about allowing visitors access to this important historic site.

This station was called Midway, as it was half way between Atchison and Denver on the old stage route. The house was built around 1850 of

Site of Diamond Springs Station, Nebraska.

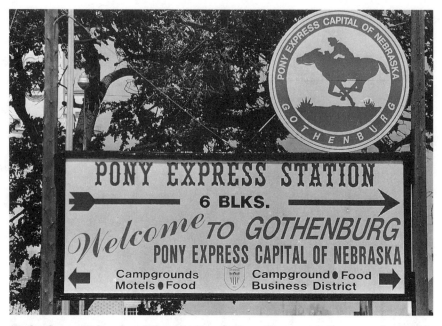

Gothenburg, Nebraska, Gilman's Ranch Pony Express station, now located in Gothenburg Park.

hand-hewn cedar logs. This was the home station for William Campbell, reputedly the last living Pony Express rider, who died in 1934. A photograph of Campbell and his wife on their sixtieth wedding anniversary hangs on one wall.

At nearby **Fort McPherson** Indian victims of the slaughter at Wounded Knee are buried.

NORTH PLATTE
(all services)

North Platte is best known as Buffalo Bill Cody's home in later life. It grew to great importance as a rail and agricultural center.

Buffalo Bill Cody, America's Greatest Western Legend

Legend has it he was an ox-team driver at age eleven, assistant wagon master at twelve; he supposedly took part in the Pike's Peak gold rush at thirteen, was one of the youngest Pony Express riders on record at fourteen, and a scout and ranger for the Union forces in the Civil War at sixteen. If we are to believe these stories, then Bill Cody managed to do more by the time he'd reached voting age than anyone else of his era accomplished in an entire lifetime.

Scout's Rest Ranch (Bill Cody's place) in North Platte.

He appears not to have slacked off much in his young adulthood. In addition to his well known exploits as a professional buffalo hunter, Cody's fame increased greatly when he reportedly killed a Cheyenne war chief named Yellow Hand in hand-to-hand combat.

Wow! No kidding? Stories of Cody's Indian-fighter days we should take with a grain of salt. Stories of his more youthful adventures require a more generous pinch. It isn't that old Bill was actually a liar. It's just that, well, he was the last person to object to the tall tales that seemed to grow up around every incident of his life.

An article in the spring 1985 issue of Kansas History presents plenty of evidence to support the claim that Cody was never more than a messenger for the Pony Express and not a rider at all. The story of Bill's 322-mile Pony Express ride (precipitated by the death of his relief rider) has long been viewed with skepticism by serious historians. But who are we to let a bunch of scholarly facts stand in the way of a good legend?

In Bill's defense it should be noted that most of the build-up of his legend was less his own doing than the embellishments of overzealous journalists and dime novelists of his day, and by a long string of biographers who were often less than critical.

In fact, the bigger-than-life Bill Cody satisfies a very basic need in the collective American ethos. We have always needed heroes, and Americans have especially wanted frontier heroes. Considering the rather low-life true character of some of the other legends of the frontier (like Duck

MAP 2: NORTH PLATTE

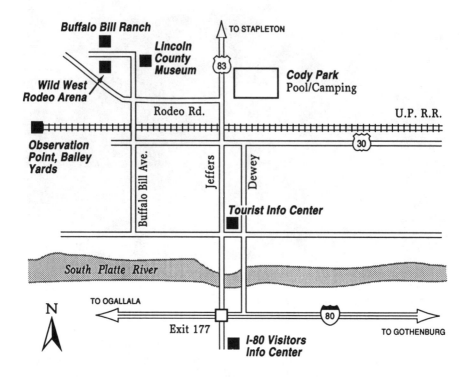

Bill, er, Wild Bill Hickok), Cody was the perfect candidate to be raised to Wild West godhood. The true measure of the man, quite apart from whatever adventures he actually did pursue in his youth and the truth (or lack thereof) of the legends that grew around him, was that he really did live up to his reputation in later life. As showman, as global ambassador, as the personification of a sort of brash and bold Western American ideal that really is larger than life, Bill Cody fit the image perfectly and today stands head and shoulders above all others in the story of the American West.

Cody built **Scouts' Rest Ranch** as his home in 1878. Today the eighteen-room mansion and show barn are part of a sixty-five-acre state historical park and present a fascinating display of the many facets of Cody's remarkable career (wink, wink!) as Pony Express rider, Indian fighter, army scout, hunter, and the greatest Wild West showman of all time. Evenings feature popular buffalo stew cookouts and cowboy sing-alongs. The park is open from late April through late October daily. Admission is by state parks sticker and an additional fee is charged for evening activities.

Other things to see and do in North Platte:

Adjacent to Scout's Rest Ranch is the **Rough Riders Rodeo** arena, featuring a nightly rodeo (summer only). Nearby is the **Lincoln County Historical Museum,** with extensive displays of western tools, weapons, and a nice recreation of a frontier railroad village (open daily Memorial Day through Labor Day, donations accepted).

The visitors' observation gallery at **Bailey Yard** gives a panoramic view of what is reputed to be the largest rail complex in the nation, the center of the Union Pacific Railroad system.

And if the kids clamor for some purely non-educational fun, head for **Cody Go Karts/Bumper Boats/Waterslide** at the junction of I-80 and US 83, where you'll find three cart tracks, three waterslides, bumper boats, and a variety of other fun rides for all ages.

During the third week of July, North Platte holds its famous NEBRASKAland DAYS celebration, featuring a four-night rodeo (across from the Cody Ranch), along with a great variety of parades, shootouts, western music, dances, and barbecues. Contact the North Platte Visitors Bureau for a detailed brochure and schedules.

There is very basic free camping in Cody Park (water but no hookups), at the corner of US 83 and Rodeo Road, and at Lake Maloney State Recreation Area (the same parks sticker required for Buffalo Bill Historical Park is good here as well), three miles south of town. For more information: Visitors Bureau, 502 S. Dewey. 1 800 955-4528; (308) 532-4729.

PAXTON

Little Paxton is the home of **Ole's Big Game Lounge,** a friendly tavern and cafe (families welcome) world famous for the former owner's two hundred hunting trophies. The food is first-rate, burgers to steaks, and as long as you're not turned off by the idea of eating in the midst of a bunch of stuffed dead animals, Ole's is well worth a stop.

The next stop on the Pony trail is wild and wooly Ogallala, which just might be the place where the West really begins.

CHAPTER FOUR

HIGH PLAINS EXPRESSWAY: OGALLALA, NEBRASKA, TO INDEPENDENCE ROCK, WYOMING

Beyond the meridian of Laramie the country totally changes. The broad prairie lands, unencumbered by timber, and covered with a rich pasturage, which highly adapts them for grazing, are now left behind. We are about to enter a dry, sandy and sterile waste of sage, and presently of salt, where rare spots are fitted for rearing stock, and this formation will continue till we reach the shadow of the Rocky Mountains.

—Burton, p. 149

OGALLALA

(all services)

Ogallala was once the terminus of the Texas Trail cattle drives, and a wild place, indeed. Known affectionately as the "Gomorrah of the Plains," it attracted scores of colorful (and mostly disreputable) characters. Today the town is considerably tamer, but it still offers a glimpse into the Wild West that was.

Ogallala's main attractions are **Front Street** and **Boot Hill.** Both are free of admission charges. Front Street is a fascinating recreation of a vintage 1880 commercial street, complete with a museum, dance hall shows at the Crystal Palace Saloon (admission charged), and evening shoot-outs. The dance hall shows are staged every evening at 8 p.m.; be ready for a shootout on the street before the show. Boot Hill is an authentic western

Boot Hill, Ogallala.

cemetery, located at West 10th and Parkhill Drive. For more information: Ogallala Chamber of Commerce, 204 East A St.

Nearby **Lake McConaughy** and **Lake Ogallala State Recreation areas** (nine miles north on Nebraska Highway 61) offer swimming, hiking, and camping. Both areas feature modern, full-service campgrounds (fees charged), and more primitive free campsites. A state parks sticker is required of all visitors.

Just to the north of Lake Ogallala, east of Kingsley Dam, is a curious memorial to religious ecumenicalism in the pioneer West. The community of Kingsley was too small at the turn of the century to support both Catholic and Protestant churches, so the townspeople built a single little chapel with a Roman Catholic altar at one end, a Protestant altar at the other, and reversible pews!

Sidetrip: Arthur/Sandhills

Thirty-six miles north of Lake McConaughy, on Nebraska 61, Arthur is the only town in Arthur County. This is real cowboy country, and one of the last places in the West where the mood of pioneer days still lingers. Arthur claims to have the smallest county courthouse in the nation. It has a church built of hay bales. For many years, Arthur's trademark has been the old cowboy boots stuck atop the fence posts lining the highway into town. A charming, peaceful place.

This is the southwest corner of one of the most starkly beautiful regions in America, the Nebraska Sandhills. The Sandhills region is the largest expanse of sand dunes in the Western Hemisphere—at 19,000 square miles, the Sandhills are about ten times the size of the state of Delaware. But this is not a desert. As the name implies, the soil is sandy, but it is stabilized by a thin covering of prairie grass. Scattered throughout the hills are hundreds of permanent, shallow lakes, springs, and creeks, and in the spring there are more than 2,000 seasonal lakes. Beneath all this is an immense underground reservoir, the Ogallala Aquifer.

This region has its own distinct topography and ecosystems, and, tied to its cattle-based economy, its own culture. Most of the rest of Nebraska was settled by pioneer farmers (a great many of them new immigrants) and resembles the farm culture of other Midwestern states. The Sandhills is definitely cattle country, and the region has much more in common with the high prairies of Montana and Wyoming, topographically and culturally.

For the vacation traveler, perhaps the greatest attraction of the Sandhills is the intriguing landscape, one of the most remarkable prairie expanses in the entire country.

See also: Sidetrips from Bridgeport, page 58.

BRULE
(limited services)

Note the colorful pioneer mural on the north side of the street in the center of this one-horse town.

JULESBURG, COLORADO
(most services)

The present town of Julesburg, built in 1881 at the junction of the Union Pacific Railroad and a spur line to Denver, is actually the fourth in a succession of Julesburgs.

The Julesburg of 1860-1861 was south of the South Platte and several miles west of the present townsite. This was an important junction, where the stage and mail traffic split: to the north, then west, along the major emigrant trails, or south to Denver and the Pike's Peak gold camps.

The town was named by Jules Reni, a powerfully built French-Canadian who ruled the place with an iron fist and the heel of his boot. Reni had been in charge of the Julesburg stage station for Russell, Majors, & Waddell and was subsequently put in charge of the Pony riders. But Reni turned out to be as dishonest as he was tough. Mail was tampered with, supplies disappeared, and the stock was not kept up to standards.

When Reni defied Majors, the company sent their superintendent for the Fort Kearny/Fort Laramie division, Jack Slade, to bring him into line.

Site of Diamond Springs Station. All photos by Joe Bensen.

Fine Victorian architecture in downtown St. Joseph, Missouri (left).

Pioneer Village, Minden, Nebraska (below).

Pony Express reenactment at Hollenberg Station in Kansas.

Ayres Natural Bridge Park, Wyoming.

Pioneer Trail Park, Salt Lake City, Utah.

Calf riding in kids' rodeo at Overton, Nebraska.

South of Evanston, Wyoming.

Pony Express/Oregon Trail marker near South Pass (Continental Divide), Wyoming.

Ruins of Hooten Wells (near site of old Desert Wells station).

Pony Express statue, outside Harrah's Stateline, Nevada.

Austin, Nevada, on US 50.

Fish Springs National Wildlife Reserve (right).

Simpson Springs Station, Utah (below).

The American River, near the site of Five Mile House Station.

Pony Express statue in Old Sacramento, California.

MAP 3: JULESBURG AREA

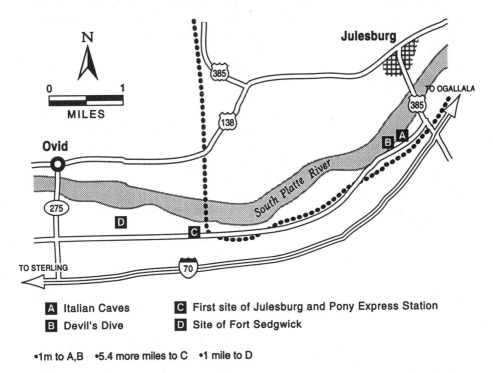

N

0   1
MILES

Julesburg

385

138

TO OGALLALA

385

Ovid

275

South Platte River

B A

D

C

TO STERLING

70

A Italian Caves   **C** First site of Julesburg and Pony Express Station

B Devil's Dive   **D** Site of Fort Sedgwick

•1m to A,B   •5.4 more miles to C   •1 mile to D

A. Italian Caves, dug by an eccentric Italian settler between 1887 and his death in 1910. Afterthe owner's death, This was a popular tourist site and picnic area for locals. It was declared unsafe and closed to the public.
B. Devil's Dive, notorious Indian ambush site. Marker for 1865 battle between U.S. cavalry and combined force of Sioux, Arapaho, and Cheyenne.
C. Site of first Julesburg and Pony Express station. Riders forded the South Platte here, striking north.
D. Site of Fort Sedgwick.

Slade had a reputation for being as rough a character as Reni, and was much more dangerous with his guns.

Reni skulked out of Julesburg, rather than confront Slade. But he returned a few days later and ambushed Slade with a shotgun. Slade was taken by stagecoach to St. Louis to have the buckshot removed from his body. One month later, he was back in Julesburg, in a most foul mood. He tracked Reni down, used him for extended, terminal target practice, and allegedly cut off his ears for souvenirs. More on the fun-loving, easygoing Jack Slade later.

Julesburg is where the young Bill Cody first worked for the Pony Express. As with most of the incidents of his life, his true career with the

Pony is obscured by layers of fiction woven by biographers more interested in telling exciting stories than recounting the truth. Depending on who you read, he was anything from a messenger boy who never actually rode the trail, to the youngest and most daring and longest-riding and so on and so forth.... In all probability, at fourteen, he would have been awfully young to have ridden at all.

A good place to start your tour of Julesburg and environs is the **Depot Museum,** on the south side of Julesburg's main street. The Depot has a small but interesting collection of pioneer and railroad artifacts, and plenty of free information about the area. Hours are Memorial Day through Labor Day: Monday through Saturday, 9 a.m. to 5 p.m.; Sunday 11 a.m. to 5 p.m. Admission is $1 for adults, $0.50 for children under 12.

Highlights of the area's history can be seen on an excellent circular drive of about twenty miles that begins and ends in Julesburg. Cross the South Platte River on U.S. Highway 385, headed south. County Road 28 departs US 385 to the west, just a few feet north of the on-ramp to Interstate 76. The first mile or so is paved, then turns to well-maintained gravel. Driving across this rolling country, it is easy to imagine the Pony riders making good time.

After 6.5 miles, you come to a marker for the original townsite and Pony Express station. After another mile there's a wooden marker on the right for the site of Fort Sedgwick, which is where much of the action depicted in the movie *Dances With Wolves* actually took place (although the filming was done in South Dakota).

Another 0.4 mile west of Fort Sedgwick is the intersection with County Road 27.8. Take this (paved) road 1.4 miles north, across the South Platte, to Ovid. In Ovid, at the corner of Main and Monroe streets, is the site of a World War II prisoner of war camp, where German POWs were housed during the beet and potato harvests. Look for the Pony Express marker at the Post Office, on the corner of Main and US 138.

From Ovid, turn back east on US 138 to return to Julesburg. About four miles east of Ovid, watch for the junction with US 385, opposite the airport. Straight takes you back to Julesburg, left takes you west and north on US 385, approximating the route of the Pony Express.

US 385 crosses back into Nebraska. Just after crossing beneath I-80, you have the option of taking the interstate twenty-six miles to Sidney or driving two-lane US 30 through Chappell and Lodgepole. The Pony Express trail ran right between the paths of these two highways.

As the trail leaves the confines of the South Platte River Valley, the rich, rolling prairie gradually turns to the rougher, wide-open, high plains. Here the farmland gives way to cattle country, and the land takes on a decidedly more "western" look.

SIDNEY, NEBRASKA

(all services)

Sidney did not yet exist when the Pony riders trotted across these grasslands. **Fort Sidney** was established here in 1867 to protect the crews that were surveying and building the railroad, and the fort played a major role in the frontier life of the region. In 1871 Fort Sedgwick was abandoned, and its garrison moved here. The rail town of Sidney boomed during the gold rush in the Black Hills, as this was the southern terminus of the famous Sidney-Deadwood Trail.

The **Fort Sidney Post Commander's Home and Officers' Quarters** at 6th and Jackson have been fastidiously restored and are maintained by the Cheyenne County Historical Association. The Officers' Quarters houses an excellent museum. Both are free. Hours are 1 p.m. to 5 p.m. daily, and 1 p.m. to 4 p.m. during winter months.

A store and free tourist attraction all in one, **Cabella's,** the well-known outfitter, is chock full of outdoor clothing and equipment and has an extensive collection of wildlife trophies. The store is just west of town on US 30. For more information: Cheyenne County Visitor's Committee, 740 Illinois St.

From Sidney, the Pony Express trail headed straight north. For today's traveler, the drive north on US 385 starts with twelve miles of blank prairie to the town of Gurley, broken only by a historical marker at mile eight on the left (west) side of the road, referring to early oil exploration in western Nebraska. There was probably a relay station at what was once a government well, just to the north and west of here.

Gurley is a fly speck on the map, and little more than a wide spot on this prairie road. There's a small cafe and a pop machine, and not much else. Dalton, six miles north, is somewhat more substantial, with basic amenities, including gas.

MUD SPRINGS STATION

(no services)

Twenty-four miles north of Sidney, watch for a sign for Mud Springs, via a well-maintained gravel road to the left (west). Follow this road 1.5 miles to another marked left turn to the station site.

The site lies within a ring of shade trees, beside a pretty pond. There is the usual stone marker with bronze plaque, a picnic table, and an outhouse, but as yet there are no modern amenities and NO WATER. This is a nice place for a picnic, but come prepared. Please remember that the adjoining ranch is private property.

Mud Springs probably served as a home station, and certainly as a stagecoach rest stop. In February of 1865, troops from Fort Laramie fought here with Indians retreating from their recent attacks on Julesburg.

Near Mud Springs Station, western Nebraska.

Nine miles north of Mud Springs turn left (west) on Nebraska 92 and rejoin the main route of the Oregon-California Trail. Today's travelers are immediately reminded of this after one mile by a marker on the north side of the road relating the numbers and causes of deaths among the emigrants.

BRIDGEPORT

(most services)

Bridgeport State Recreation Area is at the west edge of town on US 26. The area has swimming, fishing, hiking, picnicking, camping, and an RV dump station. There is no additional charge for camping with purchase of an entry permit.

Sidetrip from Bridgeport: Alliance/Carhenge

From Bridgeport it's just a forty-mile drive north (continuing on US 385) across the fringe of the great Nebraska Sandhills country to one of the kookiest and most amusing roadside attractions in the entire nation.

Carhenge is an almost exact-scale replica of Britain's famous Stonehenge, except it's built of junked cars. Jim Reinders, a Houston engineer whose family owned the farmland on which Carhenge now stands, gathered together a small group of enthusiastic pals, ponied up $12,000 of his own money, then set to work creating a work of true folk art...or a strange automotive shrine...or a vertical junkyard. Call it what you will (and locals have, over the past couple of years, called it lots of things), Carhenge is a must-see for anyone who appreciates roadside oddities. No souvenir stand, no concessions, no admission charged. It just sits there, in all its goofy and mysterious glory, in a cornfield beside US 385, 2.5 miles north of Alliance.

PONY BYWAY 1

This first of seven Pony Byway drives is entirely on paved roads, suitable for all vehicles. Because the visitor center for Chimney Rock is on Nebraska 92, it might work best to drive up to Chimney Rock, then return to Bridgeport for the Nebraska 88 drive. Otherwise, you will have to backtrack east on Nebraska 92 from Gering to visit Chimney Rock.

The turnoff for Nebraska 88 is at the southeastern edge of Bridgeport (Pony Express marker, if you're keeping score). Drive 4.4 miles south on Nebraska 88 to a marker and viewing point for Courthouse and Jail rocks.

Just past the southeastern corner of the Courthouse Rock Golf Course, where the road meets Pumpkin Creek, is the probable location of Courthouse Rock Station. At this point, Nebraska 88 swings hard right

MAP 4: NE88 DRIVE & SCOTTS BLUFF AREA

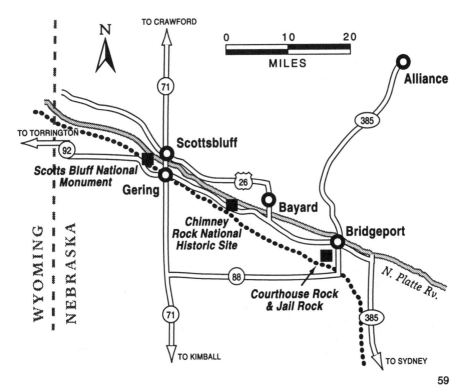

Wagon ride near Chimney Rock.

(west), presenting fine views of Courthouse and Jail rocks to the north. It is widely felt that the Pony Express route went south of these formations, while the emigrant trails ran to the north (along the river), so this drive does parallel the old trail, albeit, considerably farther south.

What Nebraska 88 really presents, however, is fifty-odd miles of wide-open spaces, on one of the finest prairie drives to be found anywhere in the United States. This is a good opportunity to catch a glimpse of the unspoiled West, and well worth the extra hour it takes. At the junction with Nebraska 71, turn right (north) and drive twenty miles to Gering and Scotts Bluff National Monument.

BAYARD/CHIMNEY ROCK

Thirteen miles west of Bridgeport on US 26, **Chimney Rock** was perhaps the first major landmark for westward travelers. Today, a small visitor center at this National Historic Site provides historic information (free). The visitor center is one mile southwest of US 26 on Nebraska 92. It is open Monday through Saturday 9 a.m. to 6 p.m., and Sunday 1:30 p.m. to 6 p.m. Try to arrive during open hours to see the informative displays of how the rock has changed in appearance over the past 150 years.

For some of the best views of the rock, look for the gravel Chimney Rock Road, on the south side of Nebraska 92, about 500 feet east of the Chimney Rock viewpoint. After about 1.25 miles this road curves to the

Group photo at Chimney Rock.

right (west) and ends after 0.25 mile at a small cemetery. Just at the big curve, don't miss the great prairie dog colony in the field to the right.

There was probably a relay station somewhere between Chimney Rock and the river, but the two most likely sites were long ago destroyed by road building and quarrying.

Howard Gordon's popular **Wagon Train Ride** is based in nearby Bayard. The three-hour trips travel along the old Oregon Trail and bring visitors close to the base of Chimney Rock. There are also evening programs with cookouts, and a variety of multi-day trips that include singing, square dancing, Indian dances, and demonstrations of pioneer skills. All trips are by advance reservation only, and prices are reasonable. Wagon trains run from May through September. Call (308) 586-1850.

Continuing west on Nebraska 92, watch for a marker for Ficklin's Springs Station on the right (north) side of the road, one mile west of Melbeta.

GERING/SCOTTSBLUFF
(all services)

This is the major population center and service area for the farming and ranching communities of the Nebraska Panhandle and much of eastern Wyoming. It's a good place to take care of shopping, car problems, and other busy work, and there are plenty of (non-Pony) attractions for the traveler.

61

In Gering, the **WYO-BRASKA Museum of Natural History** at 950 U Street contains more than 200 animal displays (many of them African), along with dioramas and dinosaur exhibits. The museum is open May 15 through September 15, Monday through Saturday 9 a.m. to 5 p.m., Sunday 1 p.m. to 4 p.m.; September 16 through May 15, Tuesday through Saturday 9 a.m. to 3 p.m.

Also in Gering, the **North Platte Valley Museum** at 11th and J streets interprets the history of settlement in this region, with an excellent example of a typical sod house, a restored log house, and twenty-one period exhibits depicting early settlement. Kids will enjoy the "hands-on" corner. Hours are May through September, Monday through Saturday 8:30 a.m. to 5 p.m. and Sunday 1 p.m.to 5 p.m.

The immense bulk of **Scotts Bluff National Monument**, towering 880 feet above the valley, was another major landmark for travelers along the North Platte River route. The visitor center has a museum featuring artifacts from the Oregon Trail and photos and paintings by William Henry Jackson. There is an interpretive hiking trail and a scenic drive with spectacular views of the valley below. Enter the monument from Nebraska 92, three miles west of Gering, five miles southwest of Scottsbluff.

Scottsbluff's **Riverside Park Zoo** has an excellent collection of indigenous and exotic animals. The Prairie Dog Community Center (with viewing bubble and tunnel) and the Petting Zoo will please the kids, while the surprising collection of African and Asian animals can be a pleasant diversion from Western travel. The zoo is at 1600 South Beltline Highway West. Hours are October 1 through April 30, 10:30 a.m. to 3:30 p.m.; May 1 through September 30, 9:30 a.m. to 4:30 p.m. (5:30 p.m. weekends).

Info Caboose. Nebraska 71 at Kings Road, Gering.

Info Caboose. US 26 at 27th Street, Scottsbluff.

From the visitor center at Scotts Bluff Monument, drive about 2.5 miles west to a detailed marker for old Fort Mitchell (probably built on the site of an earlier Pony Express station), on the south side of the road. Another 0.25 mile brings you to a T where you must turn east or west. East (right) takes you quickly back to Scottsbluff and easy access to US 26, which will be your preferred route west if time is a factor. There is another pair of Pony Express/Oregon Trail markers 0.4 mile to the east of this intersection, on the north side of the road.

If you can spare the extra half hour or so of driving, following Nebraska 92 west (left) from the intersection more closely approximates the route of the Pony Express and is quite a pleasant drive. Nebraska 92 eventually rejoins US 26 at Torrington, Wyoming, or you can rejoin US 26 at Henry by turning north (right) on the paved road from Lyman. Horse Creek Express Station stood about two miles northeast of Lyman. From here the Pony Express trail ran through what are now extensive beet fields, west into Wyoming.

TORRINGTON

(most services)

Torrington is where the emigrant trails converged with the cattle trails up from Texas. The **Homesteaders' Museum,** housed in the old Union Pacific depot, displays historical items going back to the earliest days of Torrington's settlement in the 1830s, along with prehistoric artifacts from the region. The museum is open daily in summer, Monday through Friday the rest of year. Admission is free.

Torrington's city park at West 15th and Avenue E offers free camping.

Just across the North Platte River, south of Torrington on US 85, a large marker on the left (east) side of the road designates the site of Cold Springs Station.

WYOMING TRAVEL INFORMATION

Known as the "Cowboy State" for obvious reasons, but also as the "Equality State" for being the first in the United States to allow women to vote (in 1869, while still a territory). Wyoming was also the first state to appoint a woman justice of the peace, first to select women jurors, and first to elect a woman governor.

Wyoming is the least-populated state in the nation, a place where cattle and sheep outnumber people five to one. Tourism and recreation are the state's second leading industry, after mining.

Chugwater Creek, and Fort Laramie.

Due to the lack of development along most of the old Pony Express trail through Wyoming, it is possible to drive the exact route in many places and see precisely what the riders would have experienced—well, no bandits or hostile Indians, but otherwise the landscape has changed remarkably little.

Wyoming is big on guest ranches and various sorts of western bed-and-breakfast establishments that range from rustic to elegant. Many of these are attractive for more than just an overnight stay, with hiking and horseback riding, and there is a fair concentration in the vicinity of Douglas and Casper. For information and reservations (advised) contact: Wyoming Homestay and Outdoor Adventures (WHOA!), 1031 Steinle Road, Douglas, WY 82633. (307) 358-2380.

The entrance fee for state parks is $3 per vehicle or $25 per year. Camping at most state recreation areas (generally primitive/no showers) is $4 per vehicle each night. To camp in state parks you must pay both the entrance fee and the camping fee.

FORT LARAMIE

(basic services)

Fort Laramie National Historic Site is located three miles southwest of the town of Fort Laramie, at the confluence of the North Platte and Laramie rivers. The first two forts to stand on this site, forts William and John, were important fur-trading posts between 1834 and 1849, and the first permanent institution of white endeavor on the Great Plains. In 1849 the U.S. government purchased the fort and garrisoned it with troops to protect the emigrant trails. Fort Laramie became one of the West's most important army posts and was an important stagecoach station.

By the 1880s Fort Laramie had lost its usefulness as a military post. In 1890 the fort was abandoned and the buildings auctioned. Of the original sixty-seven buildings, only twenty-two remained when it was finally designated a National Historic Site. Today, there are eleven restored buildings, with a visitor center and museum in the old commissary, and a snack bar at the old sutler's storehouse. There is a prominent monument here to the Pony Express and Overland Stage.

Fort grounds are open till dusk every day. The visitor center is open daily from 8 a.m. to 4:30 p.m. (except January 1, Thanksgiving, and Christmas Day), with hours extended to 7 p.m. from mid May till late September. On most days from early June to late August there are regular living history demonstrations (including historic weapons demonstrations), interpretive talks, and guided tours of the grounds. It is best to go immediately to the visitor center to check on programs and times. The entrance fee is $1 per vehicle.

Nearby Grayrocks Reservoir offers pleasant camping for free, but there are no facilities or drinking water. There are three commercial campgrounds in the town of Fort Laramie. Information office is on the north side of Main Street in town.

From Fort Laramie, return to town and proceed west on US 26 to Guernsey (most services), or follow Fort Laramie Road (well-maintained gravel) west across open prairie to the intersection with (paved) Guernsey Road (straight here for Grayrocks). Turn right (north) and it's a beautiful nine-mile drive to **Register Cliffs,** 1.5 miles south of Guernsey. Just at the well-marked turn-off for Register Cliffs, notice the attractive white Pony Express marker on the left, overlooking the North Platte River at the site of Nine-Mile House.

Register Cliffs are sort of a mini-Independence Rock with numerous pioneer inscriptions, as well as nearby Oregon Trail wagon ruts. There is camping at Guernsey State Park, three miles north of town.

From Guernsey/Nine-Mile House the Pony Express trail generally followed the west-by-northwest sweep of the North Platte River to the

MAP 5: TORRINGTON TO DOUGLAS

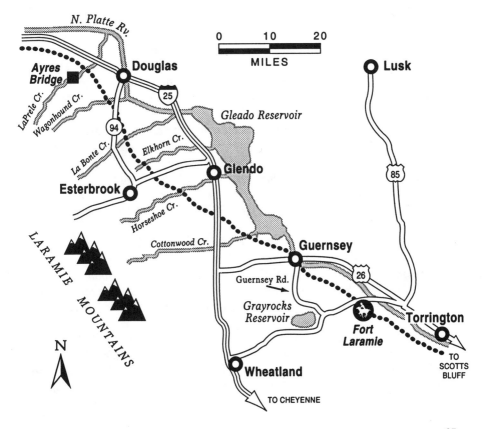

present-day city of Casper. Study the official highway map provided by the State of Wyoming and you'll see that this sweep mirrors the contour of the Laramie Mountains, to the west. A series of creeks flow east, then northeast, then north out of the Laramies, and the next eight stations (named for each creek) were located where the trail crossed each creek at right angles. In order, they were named: Cottonwood, Horseshoe, Elkhorn, LaBonte, Bed Tick, La Prele, Box Elder, and Deer Creek.

For the modern traveler, it's best to hop on I-25, fifteen miles west of Guernsey, and head for Douglas, with a possible diversion for Pony Byway #2.

The interstate crosses Horseshoe Creek just south of the Glendo exit. About five miles west of here, on the banks of this creek, stood Horseshoe Station, headquarters for one of the Pony Express's most capable division superintendents and one of the most notorious killers in the history of the American West. Nothing remains of the station, and there is no public access to the site, but it is worth considering the story of one of the Pony's most colorful characters.

Jack Slade—Baddest Dude on the Whole Trail

Jack Slade just might have been the toughest, orneriest, most dangerous man in the entire Wild West. If it had been Slade at the OK Corral instead of the Clantons, those Earp brothers and Doc Holliday would have vamoosed for New Mexico rather than face him, and Slade would have withered old Wild Bill Hickok with a glance. Legend has it he killed his first victim when he was thirteen, when he threw a rock at the head of an irate farmer whose outhouse Jack and his buddies had just tipped over. He grew to be a fearless fighter in a very hard land.

In spite of his ruthless nature (or perhaps because of it), Slade proved to be an efficient and effective district superintendent for the Pony and the Central Overland Stage Company. After Slade got rid of Jules Reni (see Julesburg entry), he took it upon himself to exterminate the nests of human vipers that inhabited the region. He was constantly on the trail between Julesburg and South Pass, in tireless pursuit of horse thieves and stage robbers.

There was little official law west of Fort Kearny. It has been said that the division superintendents for the Pony Express acted as general, judge, and jury on their sections of the trail. In Slade's case, we might add executioner. With the tacit approval of the authorities at Fort Laramie, Slade proceeded to run down and shoot lots of people, most of them bad guys.

Unfortunately, he also tended to shoot people outside the line of duty. After the demise of the Pony Express, Slade was kept on by Ben Holladay when he took over the Central Overland Stage. But Slade's legendary drinking habits, together with his violent temper, made him just too dangerous to keep on. When a friend and fellow employee went out to calm him down during a drinking and shooting spree, Slade reputedly shot him.

Site of Deer Creek Station, Glenrock, Wyoming.

Soon after, he was dismissed.

Slade supposedly killed twenty-six men, several in cold blood. He met his end, fittingly, at the end of a rope in the rough-necked Montana gold camp of Virginia City. His body was brought to Salt Lake City by his widow and buried in the old Mormon Cemetery. If you ask at the cemetery office, they will point out the location of the grave.

PONY BYWAY 2: GLENDO TO DOUGLAS

This drive is especially attractive as an early morning or evening drive. In the evening, watch for the pronghorn antelope that flourish in this environment. In fact, it is reported that seventy-five percent of the world's pronghorns live within 150 miles of Casper, so it would be unusual not to see the animals somewhere between here and South Pass.

From Glendo, there is only one road to the west, well-marked for Esterbrook. Esterbrook is just a lodge (with a restaurant) and cabins, in a beautiful spot with reportedly good fishing. There is a small USDA Forest Service campground three miles east of town.

Just north of Esterbrook the road intersects with Wyoming 94. Turn left (south) to Esterbrook, or right (north) to Douglas. About nine miles north of this intersection, the road becomes hard surface. About a mile farther along, the road climbs to a ridge after crossing La Bonte Creek. La Bonte Station stood down on the flat to the right (east), near the prominent yellow building (private property, no public access).

A few miles north of Wagonhound Creek is a county road to the left (west), marked "Bed Tick." Bed Tick Station was about four miles to the west. Douglas is about three miles farther north.

DOUGLAS

(all services)

Yet another city that wasn't around in 1861, Douglas grew up near the site of Fort Fetterman. The fort was established in 1867 at the intersection of the Oregon and Bozeman trails and named for Captain William Fetterman, who was killed in an engagement against Indians. After its abandonment by the military in 1882, Fetterman served as an informal trading post and supply center for neighboring cattle ranches, until Douglas was founded in 1886.

Fort Fetterman State Historic Site is nine miles north of Douglas, on County Road 93. The officers' quarters have been restored, and now serve as a museum. The site is open daily, Memorial Day through Labor Day, 9 a.m. to 5 p.m.

Douglas's current claim to fame is the legendary jackalope that inhabits the region. The elusive critter's image is seen everywhere in town, and the Chamber of Commerce offers free jackalope pins and jackalope hunting licenses.

There's an excellent **Wyoming Pioneer Memorial Museum** just inside the main entrance to the state fairgrounds, with many pioneer and Native American artifacts. The museum is open daily from June through September, Monday through Friday during the rest of the year. Admission is free. The Douglas fairgrounds are also home to the Wyoming State Fair the third week in August. This is a great time to catch a rodeo in real cowboy country. For fair information, call (307) 358-2398.

Douglas has one of the nicest free community camping areas in the entire West beside the North Platte River. It is clean and quiet, and even has hot showers. For more information: Douglas Chamber of Commerce, 318 1st St. W (next to the park).

From Douglas, continue west on I-25. Two exits (about ten miles) west of Douglas is the turnoff for **Ayres Natural Bridge,** a worthwhile five-mile diversion. There's an Oregon Trail marker 2.5 miles along this road. La Prele Station stood along La Prele Creek, in a pasture near a present feed lot (private property), 0.25 mile past the Oregon Trail marker, on the left (east) side of the road.

Ayres Bridge is reportedly one of only a very few natural bridges in the world that still has water flowing beneath it. The formation is 50 feet high and roughly 100 feet long. Beautiful red cliffs form a 150-foot wall at one end of the bridge. The park has picnic and playground facilities, as well as pleasant (but basic) free campsites. Ayres Park is open from April to November; the gates open from 8 a.m to 8 p.m.

Deer Creek Station stood in what is now the town of Glenrock, one of the few places in Wyoming where there is actually something to see of a former Pony Station. Look for the large metal marker—in the shape of a Pony rider—next to an auto repair shop on the east side of S. Third Street, a block and a half north of Birch (Glenrock's main east-west street). Deer Creek began as Joseph Bissonette's trading post and hostelry, and grew as an express and stage station and minor military post. This was long before the present town existed.

CASPER

(all services)

Before the Wyoming oil and uranium booms transformed Casper into the mini-metropolis it is today, the town grew as a pioneer crossing on the North Platte River, and later as a rail center.

In 1847, Brigham Young established a ferry here for the Mormon emigrants, operating it until 1852. In 1859 Louis Guinard built a trading post and bridge at the later site of Fort Caspar. Guinard's establishment also served as a stage and Pony Express stop, and as a telegraph office.

From 1862 to 1865 Platte Bridge Station grew as a military post, in response to increasing Indian hostility to the infringements on tribal lands. The post was renamed Fort Caspar for Lt. Caspar Collins, a soldier killed in 1865 in an engagement with Indians at nearby Red Buttes.

As with Kearney/Fort Kearny, there is a disagreement between the spellings of the old fort and the city that grew up around it. Again, it appears to have been a misspelling, possibly by a telegraph operator who hit a wrong key.

Today the excellent **Fort Caspar Museum** has exhibits of the old Platte River Bridge and the Pony Express, along with many exhibits on Indian and military life in the region. The museum is open daily, May to mid-September; closed Saturday during the rest of the year. Admission is free.

Accommodations at Casper

Head for the visitor center for all the details on Casper's excellent selection of motels, bed and breakfasts, and camping. There are several primitive campgrounds clustered up in the mountains about seven miles south of the city, but these are rather out of the way. Several more convenient commercial campgrounds are found in town, including one right at Fort Caspar. For more information: Visitor Center, 500 N. Center St. Open daily until 5 p.m., 7 p.m. in summer. 1 (800) 852-1889 or (307) 234-5311.

THE ROUTE WEST FROM CASPER

In some respects, Casper is as logistically important for today's traveler as it was for the pioneer emigrants. This will be the last place to take care of city business until you reach Green River or Evanston. If you do not overnight in Casper, keep in mind that accommodations are sparse

Gravel county road west of Casper—orginal Pony Express/Oregon Trail route.

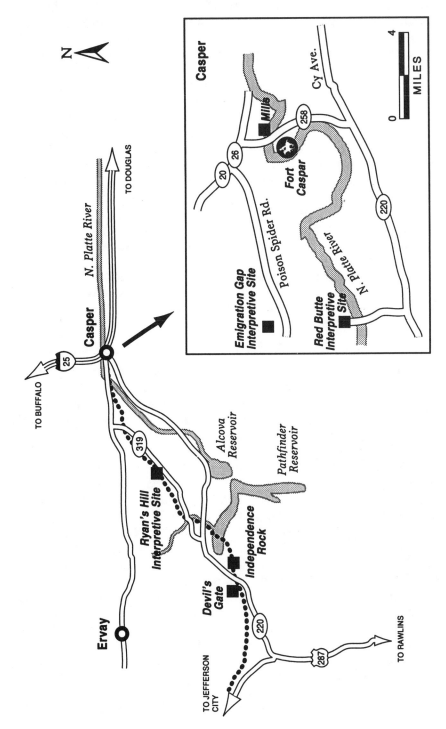

until Atlantic City or Lander. Camping is available near Alcova, Jeffrey City, and Sweetwater (junction of US 287 and Wyoming 135), and there's a small motel at Jeffrey City. If you plan to do Pony byways 3 and 4 on the same day, you must get an early start from Casper. It's perfectly driveable, but you'll be looking at a very long day that realistically won't go past Farson.

If time does not permit the following byway drive, take Wyoming 220 (CY Avenue in Casper) forty-five miles to Independence Rock. From Fort Caspar, go right (south) about one mile on Wyoming 258 to the major intersection with CY Avenue/Wyoming 220, then turn left (west).

For those who do take this faster option, be sure to visit the **Bessemer Bend/Red Buttes Interpretive Site.** Drive six miles southwest of Casper on Wyoming 220, then right for three miles on Bessemer Bend Road (well marked). Bessemer Bend was an important camping and river crossing point on the emigrant trails.

From Bessemer Bend, if you change your mind and decide to drive Pony Byway #3, you can take County Road 308 (Bessemer Road) up and to the right from the interpretive center. After 1.3 miles, turn right (north) at an obvious intersection with County Road 306 (called 12-Mile Road). Drive north four miles, turn left at the intersection with hard-surfaced County Road 202, then continue as below.

PONY BYWAY 3: CASPER TO INDEPENDENCE ROCK

This HIGHLY RECOMMENDED drive gives an excellent impression of what the Pony riders experienced, and is scheduled to be marked with BLM signs in the near future. The country here is so rough and inhospitable that it is virtually unchanged since the days of the Express. The road, although not hard-surfaced, is first-rate and will present no problems for any vehicle provided conditions are dry. This drive will add perhaps one to two hours to your driving time. Keep in mind that once you've left Casper, there will be NO SERVICES or amenities till Muddy Gap, so fill the tank, check your tires, and be sure you have food and water on board.

From Fort Caspar, head north on Wyoming 258, across the North Platte to the suburb of Mills (the last opportunity for fuel, etc.). Turn left (west) at the major intersection with Business US 20/26, then left again at the first stoplight, well-marked as Poison Spider Road.

After seven miles Poison Spider Road turns to (good) gravel. Another 1.6 miles brings you to the small Emigrant Gap interpretive site. The significance of Emigrant Gap, for both the trail pioneers and the Express riders, was that it marked the departure from the relative comfort of the North Platte River Valley to the stark high plateaus and passes of the Rocky Mountains.

From Emigrant Gap continue 1.4 miles to the intersection with 12-Mile Road from the south and (paved) County Road 202. Turn left (west) on 202 for your last bit of asphalt for the next thirty miles or so. After 1.8 miles keep your eyes peeled for County Road 319, on the left (south). With any luck the Wyoming highways department will see fit to mark this critical turnoff for travelers, as it is rather easy to miss. If you do miss this turn, you'll end up driving around the delightfully named region of Poison Spider Creek and the Rattlesnake Range. Reset your odometer here.

County Road 319 curves back to the right (west) after one mile, but the main track is obvious. From this point, it's clear sailing along what was once the old trail. Watch for the occasional gray trail markers on the north side of the road. After seven miles, there's an especially fine view from atop a hill, and you'll get a real sense of just how rough, yet starkly beautiful, this land really is.

At about mile 15.5, near the start of the climb of Ryan's Hill, is the approximate location of Willow Springs Express Station (no trace). At seventeen miles is the sign for the BLM's Ryan Hill interpretive site, 0.25 mile to the north. There are some good views of Oregon Trail wagon ruts from here.

At twenty-seven miles, where a branch road enters from the north, look for the obvious meeting of Horse Creek and Fish Creek. Horse Creek Station was probably located on the east bank of the creek. If you walk along the creek, you might spot the metal location stake driven here for the 1960 Centennial Pony Express Reride.

Three more miles brings you to Wyoming 220. The Pony trail continued south across where the highway is now, then ran through what is now Pathfinder Ranch (private), a few miles south of the highway. Turn right (west) and drive ten miles to Independence Rock.

INDEPENDENCE ROCK

(no services)

Independence Rock rises like a great gray dome out of the plains above the Sweetwater River in barren central Wyoming. The rock covers several acres and is nearly a mile around, its sloping sides polished smooth by sheets of glacial ice.

A century and a half ago this immense granite boulder was perhaps the most famous landmark and stopping place for pioneer emigrants on the Oregon and Mormon trails, thousands of whom inscribed their names on its surface. The emigrants arrived here in greatest number around the beginning of July, and the landmark was most likely named for Independence Day.

Today the rock's attraction for visitors is not its unique form, but its pioneer graffiti. Father DeSmet, the pioneer missionary, is said to have first called it "the great registry of the desert."

There is no elaborate visitor center, and no adjacent cluster of attractions and facilities—just a simple state-maintained rest area with a small information kiosk. A definite "must-see" for anyone with a real interest in pioneer history.

From the top of the rock, look back to the east about one mile to the vegetated north bank of the Sweetwater River. This is the approximate location of Sweetwater Station, near where the still-visible emigrant road joins the river. This station appears to have been on-again-off-again. When Burton came through in August of 1860, he reported it abandoned. Evidently, stations were kept at various times here, at Devil's Gate (seven miles west), and at Plante's Ranch (six miles past Devil's Gate), probably depending on who had last been burned out by Indians.

Beyond Independence Rock, we enter the Rocky Mountains in earnest.

CHAPTER FIVE

HEART OF THE ROCKIES: INDEPENDENCE ROCK, WYOMING, TO SALT LAKE CITY, UTAH

A watershed is always exciting to the traveller. What shall I say of this, where, on the topmost point of American travel, you drink within a hundred yards of the waters of the Atlantic and Pacific Oceans?

—Burton, p. 179

From Independence Rock, the Pony Express trail followed the Sweetwater River, crossing the present highway just west of the rest area, then paralleling U.S. Highway 287 to the north. **Devil's Gate Historical Interpretive Site** is 5.6 miles west of the rest area, on the right, and definitely worth a stop.

At the remote intersection called Muddy Gap (fuel and food), continue west (it's a well-marked right turn) on Wyoming Highway 789/US 287. Do NOT go left (south) to Rawlins.

Eight miles west of Muddy Gap, watch for the sign for **Split Rock Historical Site**. Three miles farther west is a monument to Split Rock Station and the Pony Express trail, which were down in the meadow below. The redoubtable Jack Slade had a real field day here, hanging two or three men (depending on the account) for murdering the station keeper.

JEFFREY CITY
(fuel, cafe, store, motel, camping nearby)
Jeffrey City was a uranium boomtown during the 1970s and early 1980s that went bust. At the peak of the boom, more than 5,000 people

lived here. If you have a spare moment, take a left (anywhere) and drive around the orderly blocks laid out for what was expected to become a thriving community. Notice the abandoned apartment houses that appear to have never been occupied. An odd and intriguing place.

Near here was Three Crossings Station. This is the place where (according to Buffalo Bill legend) the young Cody rode in from Red Buttes (seventy-six miles to the east), learned his relief had been killed, continued another thirty-six miles to Rocky Ridge, then turned back with the east-bound mochila to ride straight back to Red Buttes. Old Bill was later credited with having made "the longest ride in Pony Express history," when the 224-mile roundtrip was mysteriously inflated to 384 miles. As with all such Cody legend, this one may be a case of a twenty-gallon reputation stuffed into a ten-gallon hat.

The nearest camping is at Cottonwood, six miles east on US 287, then eight miles south on BLM road.

Be sure to stop to read the marker for Ice Slough, 9.5 miles west of Jeffrey City. Here a subterranean spring stayed frozen till late summer, giving the pioneer travelers icy relief from the hot, dusty trail. Unfortunately for today's traveler, a modern drainage canal has lowered the water level and virtually eliminated the water and ice build-up. A Pony Express station was probably a mile or so northeast of the highway, close to this point.

Highway marker for Split Rock Station.

MAP 7: JEFFREY CITY TO ATLANTIC CITY

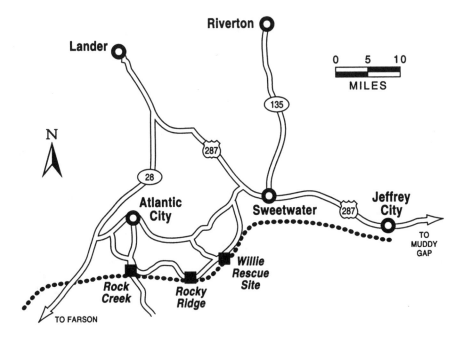

The small community of Sweetwater offers fuel, a cafe, store, and camping with showers. From here the trail ran well south of the highway.

For the modern traveler, there are three options for getting from here to Atlantic City and South Pass. In ascending order of difficulty, time, and interest: 1) continue on US 287 to the junction with Wyoming 28, then south to Atlantic City (under one hour, all on highway); 2) via the gravel Hudson-Atlantic City Road (about two hours in good conditions); 3) over Rocky Ridge, which runs closest to the actual Pony Express route (two to three hours, and sometimes rough). Low-clearance vehicles and RVs should be able to manage the Hudson-Atlantic City Road, but be sure to ask at Sweetwater about current conditions. Route option 3 is for rugged, high-clearance vehicles only.

Five miles west of Sweetwater watch for the brown wooden BLM sign for the Hudson-Atlantic City Road (2302), on the left (south). This leads to route options 2 and 3, which are both enjoyable alternatives to the highway. If you're pressed for time or want to avoid wear on your vehicle, stick to the blacktop another twenty-five miles to the intersection with Wyoming 28, then turn left (south) for twenty miles to signs for Atlantic City.

PONY BYWAY 4: OVER THE DIVIDE

The Hudson-Atlantic City Road is generally first-rate gravel, well marked and passable by most reasonably fit vehicles at moderate speeds. The road goes a bit north of where the actual trail ran, but it is extremely beautiful, wild country, and a very nice drive.

About five miles from the highway, bear right at a fork and up to the crest of a hill. From here you can see clearly where the Oregon Trail and Pony route ran, up the broad valley to the south. After four more miles there's a large BLM sign indicating twenty-two miles to Atlantic City, via the right fork.

For the adventuresome among you who really want to test your vehicle's mettle, grit your teeth and hang a left (south) here. About two to three miles south on this rough road (past a large stock reservoir), the route joins the old trail at the Willie Rescue Site. (Another road to the left (south) may be more suited to low-clearance vehicles, two miles farther along the Hudson-Atlantic City Road.)

This is the first of three monuments to the ill-fated Willie Handcart company, one of the many parties of Mormon emigrants who pushed and pulled their worldly belongings the length of the Mormon trail in light, human-propelled wagons. Through a combination of bad circumstances and poor judgment, this party found itself caught in severe winter conditions in this exposed place in October 1856. At this site, twenty-one members died of cold and starvation before a rescue party sent by Brigham Young reached them.

From this point the road leads up and over Rocky Ridge, 2.2 miles to the west. DO NOT ATTEMPT THIS IN ANYTHING LESS THAN THE STOUTEST FOUR-WHEEL-DRIVE, AND STAY OFF IT IN WET WEATHER. High clearance is essential over Rocky Ridge. If in doubt, return to Hudson Road. In fact, the Pony Express trail may or may not have crossed this ridge at all, but might have skirted it along streams to either the north or south, since a single horse could travel a roadless ravine beside a creek where wagons could not. Today's traveler, like the emigrants, must follow the high road.

At Rocky Ridge there's another monument to the Willie tragedy. Just past the marker is the roughest, rockiest section of the road. Once past this hundred-foot stretch, things improve significantly, as the road descends from the ridge. It is one mile to the first of several stock ponds below, where herds of range cattle and wild horses sometimes gather.

From the stock ponds, an interesting half-hour sidetrip can be made along what may have been a Pony Express route around Rocky Ridge, rather than over it. To the south of the first large pond is a road leading up and over a rise, then descending to where the Sweetwater runs through a pretty gorge. It is 2.4 miles from the pond to the stream, and the road is well marked with Oregon Trail and Pony Express markers, about every half mile. Near the stream is a picturesque ruined cabin, which is certainly more recent than the Pony Express (and probably a couple of miles south of where the nearest station was), but that gives a good idea of what it might have been like for the station hands and riders who manned this stretch of the trail. PLEASE KEEP IN MIND THAT THIS IS FRAGILE LAND; DO NOT LITTER OR DRIVE OFF ESTABLISHED ROADS. Return to the ponds and continue.

From the stock ponds, the trail continues west, past three more ponds and several of the now-familiar gray trail markers. About four miles past the second set of ponds, on increasingly easy road, you reach a photogenic cluster of wooden ruins that is probably the site of the town of Lewiston. Before Lewiston existed, this may have been the site of Rock Creek Station. Beyond this point, it is 4.5 miles on good road to the Willie Handcart Memorial at Rock Creek. At this place, another thirteen members of the ill-fated group perished during a snowstorm.

From here you are essentially back to civilization, with well-marked gravel roads leading to Atlantic City, South Pass City, and Wyoming 28. Head first for Atlantic City.

ATLANTIC CITY/SOUTH PASS CITY

(basic services)

Although they did not come into being until a few years after the Pony Express, South Pass City and Atlantic City offer an excellent glimpse into the pioneer and mining past of the Rocky Mountains. They lie just to the southeast of Wyoming 28 on well-marked gravel roads, and should not be missed.

Atlantic City, named for its location east of the Continental Divide, is a good example of a truly historic old mining town that is still lived-in and vibrant. Here you'll find crafts and souvenir shops, a small grocery store, and a place to sit down and have a cold drink. There's an excellent restaurant and bed and breakfast in Atlantic City—The Miner's Delight Inn (call (307) 332-3513 for reservations)—and two very attractive BLM campgrounds just outside town.

Drive four miles southwest to **South Pass City State Historic Site** from Atlantic City via well-maintained gravel roads. South Pass City is considered one of the most extensive and authentic historic sites in the West. Of the original 300 buildings, thirty remain accessible to visitors. A visitor center houses interpretive displays and a gift shop. Summer weekends are busy with numerous living history demonstrations, lectures, and films, and this place has a terrific July 4th celebration. The site is open daily, May 15 through October 15. Admission is free.

Those who took the hard-surfaced option to Atlantic City/South Pass City, might want to drive out to the **Willie Handcart Memorial,** and

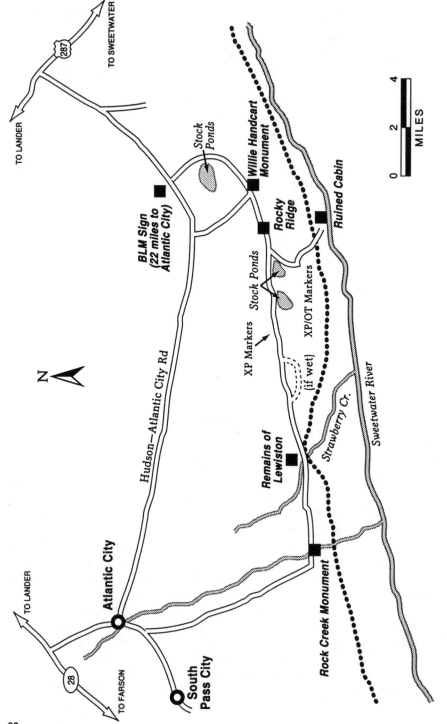

MAP 8: ROCKY RIDGE TO SOUTH PASS CITY

TO SWEETWATER

287

TO LANDER

Stock Ponds

Willie Handcart Monument

BLM Sign
(22 miles to Atlantic City)

Rocky Ridge

Ruined Cabin

MILES
0   2   4

N

XP Markers

Stock Ponds

XP/OT Markers

(if wet)

Hudson—Atlantic City Rd

Sweetwater River

Strawberry Cr.

Remains of Lewiston

TO LANDER

Atlantic City

Rock Creek Monument

28

TO FARSON

South Pass City

TO LANDER

Pony Express route markers, vicinity of South Pass.

even beyond, for an idea of what the ride was like over the beautiful high desert plains here. Even low-clearance vehicles can drive as far as the ruins of old Lewiston without difficulty.

Sidetrip: Lander
(all services)

About thirty-five miles north of Atlantic City/South Pass City on Wyoming 28/US 287, Lander is the commercial hub for this region and is thus a good bet for overnight facilities, car repair, and other essentials. Lander is also home to several guided recreational companies. The views from the highway north of the intersection of Wyoming 28/US 287 are spectacular. For more information: Lander Chamber of Commerce, 160 North 1st Street.

Most of the pioneer travel through this region (including the Pony Express route) followed the approximate route of Wyoming 28 south and west from the Continental Divide at South Pass, toward the present town of Farson.

To visit the actual site of the **South Pass watershed,** one of the most important places in the history of travel and exploration in North America, continue southwest on Wyoming 28 from South Pass City. At the crest of the first hill beyond the Sweetwater River (rest area), watch for Oregon Buttes Road on the left (south). Follow this 2.8 miles to the historical marker. From here you may hike (over easy terrain) one mile to South Pass Summit and additional markers.

Return to Wyoming 28. Watch for a group of Oregon Trail markers 10.2 miles south of Oregon Buttes Road. Near here (actually, eight miles west) a major branch of the Oregon Trail took off due west. This is also approximately where the Express riders crossed the present-day highway. From here the Pony Express trail ran parallel to the highway, across the plains to the right (northwest).

FARSON
(basic services, limited motel rooms)

Farson is essentially a crossroads with a cluster of basic services for the surrounding region. Big Sandy Pony Express station was located here, but its exact site (somewhere along the banks of the Big Sandy, possibly near the Latter Day Saints church) is unknown.

From here the Pony riders had a fast ride across open land to the southwest, generally paralleling Wyoming 28 along the left (south) side of the road.

Cross Big Sandy Creek (do NOT turn south on US 191) and note markers for the Pony Express and Oregon and Mormon trails on the west side of the bridge. Ten miles along Wyoming 28 is a memorial to an incident in the short-lived Mormon War of 1857. Two miles farther is a nice interpretive site for the Oregon Trail and telegraph. If you look off to the southwest, the Big Timber Express Station was about three miles away, on the north bank of Big Sandy Creek.

Just 1.7 miles west of the interpretive site is an obvious junction with a county road, well marked to the left (south). This road parallels the highway and follows the route the riders took. It makes a pleasant short alternative to the asphalt, and offers easy return to the main road at various obvious places.

Approximately twenty-five miles west of Farson, Wyoming 28 crosses the Green River. Green River Station stood on the west bank. The BLM is currently building an interpretive site here for the old Lombard Ferry that carried emigrants across the river.

Also here is **Seedskadee National Wildlife Refuge.** The refuge is home to more than 170 species of birds during various migratory seasons, and makes a pleasant short stop.

Continue to the intersection with Wyoming 372. Turn left (south) and drive twenty-seven miles to I-80 (all services in Green River, six miles east). From here take the interstate west toward Fort Bridger. There was a Pony Express station, called Ham's Fork, in the present town of Granger, where a plaque and several ruined buildings mark what may have been the actual site. Granger is a five-minute sidetrip; take US 30 (exit 66) north five miles.

Sidetrip: Green River/Flaming Gorge National Recreation Area

Green River is the gateway to 201,000 acres of dramatic landscape centered around Flaming Gorge Lake. The lake boasts some 375 miles of shoreline, with multi-colored sandstone cliffs in some places 1,500 feet high.

An excellent 160-mile loop drive of the entire lake area can be made on Wyoming 530, US 191, and Utah 44, with a stop at the visitor center at Red Canyon Vista. Boats can be rented at Buckboard Crossing, and camping is available at numerous points along the loop drive.

Stop in the town of Green River at the Flaming Gorge Visitor Center, on Uinta Drive south of the River (follow the signs across the only bridge in town).

FORT BRIDGER STATE HISTORIC SITE

Fort Bridger was built in 1842 by the famous mountain man, Jim Bridger, and his partner, Louis Vasquez. The fort and trading post was second only to Fort Laramie in importance as a supply point for pioneer emigrants.

In 1857, in response to increasing friction between the new Mormon settlements to the southwest and the federal Government, President Buchanan sent U.S. troops to the area, thus starting the "Mormon War." The Mormons burned Fort Bridger, which was subsequently rebuilt as a military post. Through the 1860s, the fort served as an important stage-coach and Pony Express station, and its position along the route of the advancing railroad later made it an important supply center. The fort was abandoned in 1890.

This is a real must-see for anyone interested in life on the American frontier. There is a well-curated museum in the restored barracks, along with frequent interpretive events and craft demonstrations. Grounds are open daily, 8 a.m. to sunset. The museum is open May through October, daily; weekends only during the rest of the year; and is closed December 1 through February 28. The entry fee is $1 per vehicle. The site offers a picnic area and limited camping. A four-day Mountain Man Rendezvous is held here Labor Day weekend, with Native American dancing, black-powder shoots, and many exhibits.

Fort Bridger also marks the final separation of the Oregon Trail and the old Pony route. From here west, the Pony trail followed the old Mormon Trail into the Salt Lake Valley, and westward along the trail used by some of the Forty-Niners to reach the California goldfields.

EVANSTON

(all services)

Evanston began as a crew camp for the Union Pacific Railroad in 1868—yet another place that didn't exist at the time of the Pony Express—and the town's early history was very much tied to the railroad. In more recent years, Evanston benefitted from Wyoming's oil boom, then suffered somewhat in the 1980s bust.

If you happen to be here on a Thursday, the town band gives concerts in downtown Martin Park (across from the post office) from 7 p.m. to 8 p.m. Bear River Travel Information Center is off Interstate 80 East at exit 6.

Bear River Station was located on a ranch still owned by the Myers family in a pretty valley south of Evanston. The site itself is on private property, but the ranch, along with the entire valley that the riders traversed, can be seen from high points along the county road.

Take Wyoming 150 south from Evanston about seven miles. The road will curve hard to the left, then hard to the right. Just at this second curve, watch for the county road on the right (west). This road stays high along the southern bench of the valley, which spreads out below. The Mormon Trail, Overland Stage, and Pony Express all followed this valley westward. Just as the road starts to descend, as the valley floor widens and the trees along the river disappear, note the Myer's ranch—the old station site—just beyond.

Young rodeo cowboys, Evanston, Wyoming.

MAP 9: EVANSTON/BEAR VALLEY TO SALT LAKE CITY

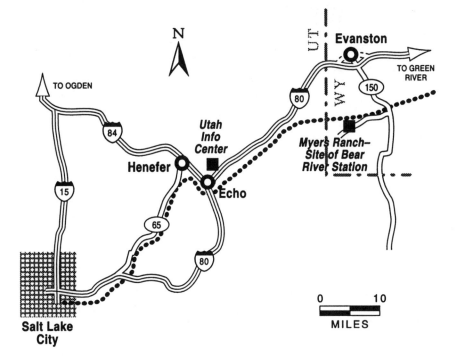

Return to Evanston and rejoin I-80. About twelve miles west of the Utah line, at the Castle Rock exit, note the junkyard on the right, about 300 yards north of the highway. This was the site of Castle Rock (or Head of Echo Canyon) Station. Nothing remains of the old station, and the junkyard and ranch are private property (with a very mean dog!).

Echo Canyon was the route for the Pony Express and Overland Stage, as well as for the Mormon pioneers and California Trail emigrants. Of his trip through Echo Canyon, Burton wrote (p. 207):

> "We longed for a thunder-storm: flashing lightning,
> roaring thunders, stormy winds, and dashing rains—in fact a
> tornado—would be the fittest setting for such a picture so
> wild, so sublime as Echo Kanyon."

This is another of those places where it's obvious the ride was easier in one direction (west and downhill) than the other. There may have been a relay station called Halfway, just seven miles down canyon from Castle Rock, although its location is unclear. At any rate, the Pony Express route was approximately that of the present highway, 16.8 miles to the town of Echo. Be sure to stop at the excellent **Utah Information Center,** just before the Echo exit.

Echo, Utah, site of Weber Station.

Weber Station was at what is now the northwest edge of the town of Echo, just below where the old highway curves around the prominent sandstone prow, on land that is now private property. A famous landmark, Pulpit Rock, once loomed above the station site, but was blasted away when the old highway was built. The station house originally served as a general store, saloon, inn, blacksmith's shop, livery, and jail. Nothing remains but some rough foundation walls, as the building was torn down in 1931.

UTAH TRAVEL INFORMATION

Although the region had been explored by trappers and Spanish missionaries, it was the Mormon followers of Brigham Young who first settled the land. In casting about for a new Zion for his fellow fugitives from eastern communities inhospitable to the Church of Jesus Christ of Latter Day Saints, Young was said to have remarked: "If there is a place on this earth that nobody else wants, that's the place I am hunting for." So he ended up with Utah, which turned out to be not such a bad deal after all.

At the time of the Pony Express, Utah was almost exclusively a Mormon enclave. During the great Mormon migration of 1847, more than 1,600 Mormon pioneers settled in Utah. By the time the Pony ran, there were more than 4,000 Latter Day Saints living here and in neighboring Nevada.

This has always been a place where topography, soil conditions, and water (or lack of it) have dictated where humankind can or cannot live, and huge regions of the state are still devoid of habitation. In fact, nearly seventy-five percent of Utah's 1.8 million citizens live within fifty miles of Salt Lake City.

Here you will find perhaps the best variety of truly outstanding wilderness landscapes of any single state. Although best known for its magnificent southern sandstone deserts and canyons, Utah is also graced with tremendous alpine terrain across the northeast portion of the state, and extremely rugged desert plains in the west.

Utah has arguably the best developed tourism industry in the nation; indeed, tourism and recreation is the state's leading industry. There is so much to see and do here, any traveler's first stop on entering the state should be the excellent Utah Travel Council visitor center, two miles east of the junction of I-80 and I-84, about twenty-seven miles west of the Wyoming line.

Recommended Sidetrip

None of Utah's several marvelous national parks lie along the Pony Express route. If time permits, a sidetrip to Zion, Bryce Canyon, Capitol Reef, Arches, or Canyonlands national parks is highly recommended. For more information on these and other Utah attractions, visit a Utah Travel Council Information Center (on I-80 at Echo Canyon or in Salt Lake City at Council Hall), or stop in at the Salt Lake City Visitor Information Center, 180 Southwest temple, phone: (801) 521-2868.

From Echo, take I-84 west five miles to Henefer. At a point about two miles west of Echo, the trail crossed the Weber River and went up and over the Wasatch Range to the west. In bad weather the riders continued on to the Brimville Emergency Station (at present-day Henefer), then followed the old Mormon Trail west, which is the same as today's Utah 65. (Note: Utah 65 is closed during winter, when the alternative is to continue on I-80 west from Echo to Salt Lake City.) Drive through Henefer to the sign for East Canyon Recreation Area (Utah 65). Turn left and drive up excellent road through attractive rangeland, then a short descent to East Canyon Reservoir. Several monuments to the Mormon emigrants line this road. East Canyon Station (also called Dixie Hollow) was somewhere beneath the present-day reservoir. There is camping at the Recreation Area, as well as at two national forest campgrounds farther down the west side of the range.

Just south of the reservoir is a monument for Bauchmann's Station, although experts still debate over the exact location of this site. Six miles west of the reservoir, up through pine forests and lovely aspen groves, the road arrives at Big Mountain Pass, with several trail markers and a great view to the west. There are two very basic national forest campgrounds on the descent west of the pass.

Near the entrance to the Mountain Dell Recreation Area is a monument for Ephraim Hanks Station. Follow the road down Emigration Canyon, to **Pioneer Trail State Park,** just inside the environs of Salt Lake

City. Pioneer Trail Park honors the Mormon emigrants and has nothing to do with the Pony Express, but it is an essential introduction to the early settlement of the Salt Lake Valley (open daily, June through September).

SALT LAKE CITY

(all services)

In addition to being the Mormon version of Rome, Salt Lake is the best tourist town in the entire Intermountain West. In terms of sheer variety of things to see and ease of getting around, this might be the most visitable city in the entire nation.

First stop for all visitors should be the Visitor Bureau on West Temple Street. Beyond that point, take your pick, depending on time and preference. One site that should not be missed, however, is the visitor center at **Temple Square.** Religious propaganda? Well, sure, it probably is. But it's much more than that. The history of Utah is tied directly to the history of the Church of Jesus Christ of Latter Day Saints, and the exhibits here tell these stories in a most engaging fashion. And don't worry about religious hard sell; you won't get it from the friendly, tactful LDS volunteers here. The Temple Square visitor center is free and open daily, with guided tours.

The Pony Express and Central Overland stage maintained a station at what is now 143 South Main Street. This is one of the few places where the Pony riders actually trotted down the main street of a substantial community. The monument has been moved slightly to the south, where it's interesting to watch the daytime throngs pass by unaware of the history in their midst.

There are all manner of accommodations to choose from in Salt Lake City, with a fair selection of reasonably-priced motels on North Temple Street, stretching west from Temple Square. As with all large metro areas, camping is less convenient. There are KOA and CAMP VIP campgrounds (both open year-round), next door to one another, fourteen blocks west of Temple Square on North Temple Street. And an extremely attractive national forest campground is at Tanner's Flat, about eight miles up Little Cottonwood Canyon, on the road to Alta/Snowbird. There are no services, no hookups, and no showers, and it's a solid half-hour drive from downtown, but Tanner's Flat can be a cool, quiet relief from the valley below.

For eating, try **Lamb's Grill** at 169 South Main Street, Salt Lake City's oldest restaurant. This place appears not to have changed since the 1920s, and exudes a unique atmosphere of tradition and gentility. The food measures up to the ambience. Attire here is semi-formal; you don't need a jacket or tie, but you might feel out of place in shorts. Try to avoid the midday lunch hour, as this place is popular with the Salt Lake business community. For more information: Salt Lake Convention & Visitor Bureau, 180 SW Temple Street.

CHAPTER SIX

MILES FROM NOWHERE: SALT LAKE CITY, UTAH, TO FORT CHURCHILL, NEVADA

*Sand Springs Station deserved its name.... The water near
this vile hole was thick and stale with sulphury salts: it
blistered even the hands. The station house was no unfit
object in such a scene, roofless and chairless, filthy and
squalid, with a smoky fire in one corner, and a table in the
center of an impure floor, the walls open to every wind, and
the interior full of dust... Of the employees, all loitered and
sauntered about desoeuvres as cretins, except one, who lay
on the ground crippled and apparently dying by the fall of a
horse upon his breast bone.*

—Burton, p. 548

The roughest, most dangerous stretch of the entire Pony Express trail
ran straight across western Utah and Nevada. The numerous small
mountain ranges of the Great Basin extend generally north to south, presenting physical obstacles for the riders to cross. Freshwater springs tend
to be seasonal, and streams, where there are any, can just end in evapo-
ration "sinks" in the desert. Naturally, in such a wasteland, there was
little permanent habitation between Camp Floyd in Utah and the Carson
Valley in western Nevada.

The Pony Express trail strikes across the Great Basin, a barren,
starkly beautiful region between the west slope of the Rocky Mountains
and the east slope of the Sierra Nevada. In prehistoric times, the eastern
half of this huge desert wasteland was filled with a gigantic inland salt-

Sand Mountain Recreation Area, Nevada.

water sea, known as Lake Bonneville. This lake was 145 miles wide and 350 miles long, filling most of the western half of Utah from the Wasatch Front into what is now eastern Nevada. The Great Salt Lake, Sevier Lake, Utah Lake, and the Bonneville Salt Flats are remnants of this vast inland sea.

Rough as this section is, it is perhaps the most interesting for today's traveler. As with the Pony riders, travelers today will find easy driving across the desert valleys and rougher going across the north-south mountain ranges.

This entire region can be blistering hot in summer, arctic cold in winter. For those taking advantage of the numerous opportunities to get off the highway and drive along desert roads, be advised that rain and spring thaw can make conditions very difficult. Inquire locally about road conditions, and stay off the dirt tracks after even the lightest rain.

When traveling in desert country, please keep in mind the special fragility of these dry lands. While this may seem a brutal, barren wasteland, it is, in fact, extremely susceptible to damage and it does not heal as easily as less arid land. Man-made refuse (even organic litter) does not disintegrate readily in the desert, and desert soil is easily damaged by vehicle tracks.

ROUTE OPTIONS FROM SALT LAKE CITY

No modern highway parallels the precise route of the old Pony Express trail from Salt Lake across western Utah and into Nevada. From about the middle of Nevada westward, U.S. Highway 50 is pretty close to the old trail, but from Salt Lake to near Eureka, Nevada, people who wish to travel along the old trail will have to make an effort and be a little adventuresome.

For travelers in a hurry, perhaps the best option is to simply scoot down Interstate 15 to the intersection with US 6, then take this good two-lane highway through Eureka to Delta (where US 6 joins US 50), and on to Nevada. This is, in fact, a wonderful drive in its own right, providing opportunities to visit the fascinating Tintic mining district (south of Eureka) and the new Great Basin National Park (near Baker, Nevada), as well as some of the best desert scenery to be seen from any hard-surfaced road. But this route runs considerably south of the old Pony Express route, so don't expect to see any references to the old trail.

SALT LAKE CITY TO LEHI

(drive directly on I-15, or stop to see the following two sites)

From Salt Lake City the Pony Express trail closely parallels I-15. As you head south from Salt Lake, you might want to visit the site of Travelers Rest stagecoach and Pony Express station, although there's not much to see. Exit at Murray (5400 Street S.) and turn left (north) on State Street.

MAP 10: SALT LAKE CITY TO CARSON CITY

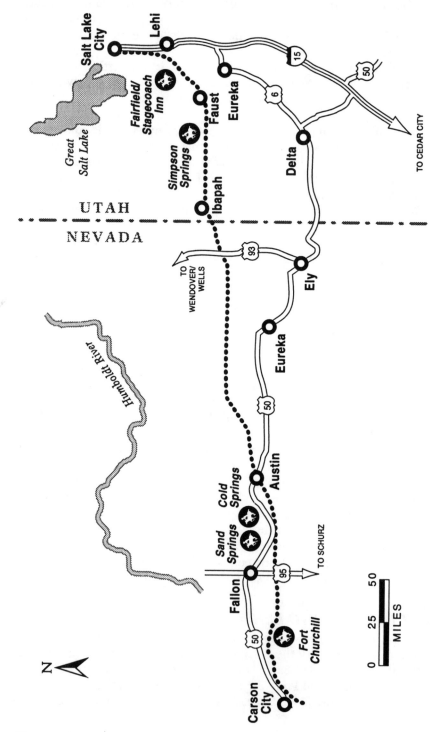

Half a block north of 5300 S., on the right (east) is a small streetside park with an attractive stone monument, but little else. Now back to I-15.

At the Bluffdale/State Prison exit (number 291), real station hounds may want to see the site of the station run by the famous Mormon gunfighter, Porter Rockwell. Rockwell had been one of Brigham Young's bodyguards and served as Territorial Marshall for Utah in the 1850s. Exit I-15, turn right at the sign for the state prison (note that you are on "Pony Express Road"), then left at the sign for the historical monument. The marker sits beneath a shade tree, just outside the state prison compound. You can continue to Lehi on Pony Express Road, or return to I-15.

LEHI
(last full-service community for a long way)

Lehi is an attractive old community, with plenty of pioneer-era things to see if you have a spare hour or so. A walking and driving tour map of historic attractions is available at the Hutchings Museum of Natural History, 685 North Center Street. Center Street is the main north-south thoroughfare in Lehi; Main Street runs east-west and becomes the Pony Express route for modern travelers.

MAP 11: LEHI TO FISH SPRINGS

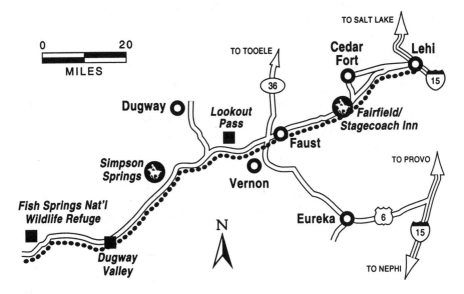

Pronghorn antelope.

PONY BYWAY 5: LEHI—SCHELLBOURNE

Actually, this shouldn't be a byway option at all, but the recommended route for all but the most rushed travelers. From Lehi, the trail struck west via Camp Floyd and the Fish Springs Range, to the present-day hamlet of Ibapah, then across what later became the Goshute Indian Reservation and on to Schellbourne (spelled variously with or without the c), at the crossing of modern US 93.

Although mostly dirt and gravel, the roads as far as Schellbourne are well-maintained and perfectly driveable in any vehicle, provided roads are dry. And because this stretch of the old trail is so beautiful, so interesting, and so well marked, it is well worth the dust and slower driving speeds to stick closely to this route.

A WARNING, however, is in order for those who are not carrying camping gear: it's a long haul westward from Lehi to the nearest full-service town. Leave Salt Lake City early (certainly by 9 a.m.) if you want to reach Ely by dark. There's a small RV park in Ibapah, but no rooms between Lehi and Schellbourne (about 300 miles), and very limited accommodation in the latter.

Because the campsite at Simpson Springs is so attractive, campers may find an early afternoon start from Salt Lake City is a realistic option. Do keep in mind, however, that fuel, food, and water are scarce for the next 200 miles, so no one should go beyond Lehi without supplies. And even though the roads between here and Schellbourne are first-rate, there will be little opportunity for assistance in the event of a break-down. Check your spare, your belts and hoses, and if you don't trust your vehicle, think about skipping the desert drive.

Main Street becomes Utah Highway 73, headed west (there's an excellent bakery at the west end of Main). After 2.5 miles you'll have a chance to "cross over Jordan"—Utah's Jordan River, that is. A relay station called Dorton's Dugout was built in a depression near the top of a small hill at Nine Mile Pass, between Lehi and Cedar Fort. Cedar Fort has a gas station.

FAIRFIELD/CAMP FLOYD AND STAGECOACH INN STATE PARK

Fairfield lies twenty miles west of Lehi on Utah 73. Just before the Civil War, one of the largest troop concentrations in the entire country was garrisoned at Camp Floyd in fear of a Mormon uprising. At its height, Fairfield had a population of 7,000 (3,000 of them soldiers). It must have been a wild place, with its seventeen saloons.

Stagecoach Inn, a popular stage stop and Pony Express station, now serves as a visitor center for a state park. This is the original building, built in 1858 and operated by the Carson family until 1947. A nice spot for a picnic, it's open daily from Easter through mid October. A small entry fee is charged.

Just east of Fairfield is a shot-up BLM sign. Seems the local chapter of Gun Nuts R Us just can't resist peppering such a colorful target with a few "30-06 kisses." In fact, virtually everything man-made you see along this road (which isn't much, anyway) has been shot full of holes. Oh well, to the marksmen's credit at least most of the bullet holes are dead-center....

Five miles west of Fairfield leave Utah 73 (and the asphalt) at the well-marked turn on the left for Faust, via the old Pony Express route. There's a fair chance that between here and Callao you'll get closer to an army helicopter in flight than you've ever been before, due to the proximity of several military facilities.

Watch for the small Scenic Byway markers put up by the BLM. They're rather narrow, perhaps because this makes them harder for the local marksmen to hit. There are also plenty of the familiar gray Pony Express markers, usually to the left (south) of the road, and mostly well-perforated—rather picturesque, in a Wild West way.

At six miles, watch for the Rush Valley Station marker (nicely shot-up, of course) on the right. Look past the marker to the north and notice the odd complex of military bunkers. It is intriguing to ponder what sorts of top-secret activities might go on in such an elaborate facility, in such a remote location.

After another 5.6 miles the road crosses a railroad line, and one mile farther arrives at the charming cluster of mobile homes and ramshackle wooden barns that constitute Faust, at the junction with Utah 36.

Turn left (south) on Utah 36 and drive 0.5 mile to a well-marked turnoff to the right (west). Actually, this is over-marked, with no fewer than five signs indicating the traveler should hang a right, so if you miss this turn you deserve to end up in Vernon, Utah (fuel, water, convenience store). As a final landmark for this turn, note the quaint little shack with the big letters, BEER, on the left.

After 1.8 miles is a BLM interpretive site for the actual Faust Station (only slightly shot-up in 1993). Five miles past the BLM site begins the easy climb to Lookout Pass. From the pass, there's a good view to the west of the desert that was called "Paiute Hell." During the 1870s, Horace Rockwell (Porter's brother) and his wife Libby occupied what had earlier been a Pony Express station, on the west side of the pass, 0.75 mile in descent. There is no trace of the cabin, but nearby is a marker for a cemetery where Libby buried her pet dogs.

Take the well-marked left fork, 3.7 miles west of Lookout Pass and, *oh boy, we're in the desert now!* This is a wild, rugged, exciting landscape. It seems foreign, like it could be the Australian outback or Africa's Rift Valley, and it's a little amazing that this close to major roads and urban areas one can feel so far away from the modern world. Even today, the place seems so remote. Except for the speed one travels along the good gravel road, this leg of the journey is little changed from the days of the Express.

There may have been a relay station about eight miles west of Lookout Pass, at a place called Government Creek where later there was a telegraph station. There's no mention of it in contemporary reports, but the gap between Lookout Pass and Simpson's Springs seems too great, since stations appear to have been spaced every eight miles in this rough region.

Simpson Springs Station is 16.5 miles west of Lookout Pass. One of the few places in Utah's western desert where there was plentiful water, this was an important station from the time of Chorpenning's Jackass Mail.

Today there is a fine reconstructed stone building (probably 300 feet east of the actual site), and a very attractive BLM campsite. The water here is unsafe to drink, so bring plenty of your own, especially if you plan to camp. This is a great place to spend the night if you want to experience the remoteness of the region, which is accentuated after sundown. Sunset behind the Dugway Range can be really spectacular.

Eight miles west of Simpson Springs is a monument to Riverbed Station, long-since disappeared. Approximately 8.5 miles past Riverbed is a fork to the left (south)—look for a water tank and ancient watering trough. (This fork was unmarked in 1993.) For the Pony route, go

MAP 12: FISH SPRINGS TO SHELLBOURNE, NV

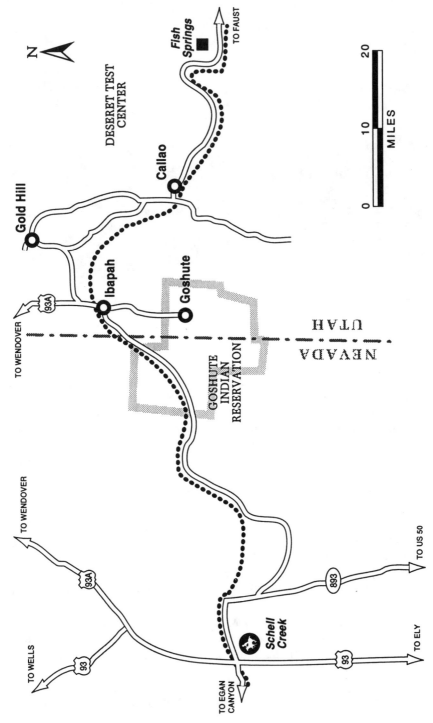

Simpson Springs Station.

straight (west), toward the Dugway Mountains. Although ardent site collectors and monument aficionados may want to take the left fork to visit the site of Dugway Station, trust me, there's not much to see. In fact, there never was much here, even when the Pony ran. Burton described the station as "a hole, four feet deep, roofed over with split cedar trunks and with a rough adobe chimney. Water had to be brought in casks." If you insist on visiting this site, go 1.5 miles south to a rough track on the right (west) posted with a Pony Express marker. The monument is 0.8 miles along this track, which is passable by car, with care. Return to the main road.

About 1.25 miles west of the watering tank and trough, if you look about a mile due south, you can just barely see the monument for Dugway, a tiny black dot in the desert. Pause a moment to contemplate the hardships and dangers faced by the daring express riders, and to feel smug about the time and trouble you saved by not driving down there to see Dugway up close....

The climb into the Dugway Mountains begins after another mile or so. The road bed on the ascent is rougher than down on the desert floor, but neither the road nor the climb should present problems for any reasonable vehicle.

From the pass you'll get your first glimpse of the alkali desert wastes to the northwest. That white wasteland in the distance is part of the U.S.

In the desert west of Simpson Springs.

Army's Dugway Proving Grounds and it's probably a good thing that, even if you wanted to drive into it, you can't. The Pony Express trail ran just to the north of the present road. At 7.5 miles from the fork to Dugway Station, note the road on the right (north) to the Dugway Geode Beds.

A monument (badly vandalized in 1993) for Black Rock Station is on the right, about fifteen miles from Dugway Fork. A few miles farther, you will enter **Fish Springs National Wildlife Refuge** (admission is free). Follow the signs to the refuge headquarters, then 0.8 miles farther to a monument for Fish Springs Station.

Fish Springs is a true desert oasis, and a birdwatcher's paradise. The refuge contains a 10,000-acre spring-fed marsh criss-crossed by roads built on dikes, and is especially rich in ducks, heron, and egrets. Keep in mind that while there's plenty of bird life to see here, there are virtually no services.

From Fish Springs, the Pony Express trail went over the pass just south of the station, while the stage and wagon route was the same as the present road; there are plenty of concrete markers to the right (north) of the road. Eight miles west of Fish Springs, note the old mine workings on the left. At **Boyd's Station**, thirteen miles west of the Fish Springs monument, there is a BLM interpretive site and one of the best-preserved stations in Utah. Callao is nine miles farther west.

A backcountry byway west of Simpson Springs, Utah.

CALLAO

(no services)

After about a mile of meandering past picturesque old cabins and corrals, there is a marker on the right, outside the Bagley ranch, for the site of Willow Springs Station (private property). Actually, there is some debate over precisely where this station was located, since contemporaneous written accounts by Burton and one of the local Pony riders do not describe the popularly accepted site. It is likely there might have been more than one station site in this well-watered area.

From the Willow Springs monument drive 0.5 mile to a well-marked intersection and turn right (north). At six miles from Willow Springs, note the ranch off to the left, where there might have been a station (what Burton refers to as "Mountain Springs"). Thirteen miles from Willow Springs is the excellent BLM **Canyon Station Interpretive Site** and ruins of a round fortification built in 1863 just west of the site of Canyon Station. It is fourteen miles from here to Ibapah. The road deteriorates somewhat, but is still fine for two-wheel-drive vehicles. An old Civilian Conservation Corp monument for Burned Out Station can be seen west of the road, 3.5 miles past Canyon Station ruins.

IBAPAH

(basic services)

Just before Ibapah look for an odd red octagonal marker, where you'll turn left on a road covered with smooth black stuff. At least, that's how it may seem to you after the past 125 miles. If you turn right here, you're on the asphalt escape route to US 93, about twenty-five miles to the north; (Wendover, Nevada, is one hour north, with all services). Don't abandon the Pony Express trail here unless you've absolutely had it with desert driving or you're caught by dark—the route ahead to Schellbourne is on very good dirt roads.

Ibapah Trading Post, one mile north of town, is the actual site of Deep Creek Station, the home station for Howard Egan, Division Superintendent between Salt Lake and Roberts Creek (near Eureka, Nevada). The Trading Post is primarily a private ranching enterprise, although they do run a general store and gas station and have one (sometimes two) simple rooms to rent.

In the thriving metropolis of Ibapah, the Deep Creek Pony Express Stop convenience store has fuel, phone, a decent assortment of groceries, and microwave food (and really cool souvenir Pony Express T-shirts!). They also run an RV park, and hope to add a few cabins in the not-too-distant future.

At the south end of town are clear signs for 8-Mile, Nevada, and the Pony Express route, via a gravel road on the right. This road starts out a bit rough, but soon turns into a veritable gravel superhighway.

Half a mile on the right is a Civilian Conservation Corps monument, somehow misplaced. At mile 5.6 you will enter the Goshute Indian Reservation. At mile 7.2 (the approximate location of 8-Mile Station) keep to the right at the unmarked fork. This will bring you out into broad, treeless Antelope Valley.

This valley is nearly fifteen miles wide. Look across the valley to a small dark patch of trees: that's Tippet's Ranch. All sorts of roads and rough tracks criss-cross the valley, and it's virtually impossible to get lost in this huge, open plain. Just wend your way across to the west side, using the dark oasis of Tippet's as your northern reference.

About 6.5 miles west of 8-Mile, note the Pony Express sign about 100 yards down the left (south) fork. This track presents a good photo opportunity, especially early in the morning. You can follow this track across the valley to Antelope Springs, but the good graded road will save wear and tear on your vehicle.

On the west side of the valley, the main road angles left (south), past the solitary ranch site. About 2.5 miles south of Tippet's watch for a Pony Express trail marker and the sign for Antelope Springs up the dirt track to the right (west). The site of the old station is in the vicinity of the stock pond 1.5 miles up this road. Nothing remains but the view. This track over the Antelope Range is the actual trail and the shortest route to

Schellbourne, but it's rough going above the pond, so it will be quicker and easier to stick to the graded road that skirts these hills to the south. This is a perfect example of why the Pony Express route sometimes differed slightly from the stagecoach route and the emigrant trails: a horse could cross terrain that wagons and coaches could not.

Continue south 9.7 miles from the Antelope Springs turnoff, then take the obvious right fork. This road heads west, then north, then west again, for five miles, where it intersects a north-south road (Nevada 893) at a stop sign and BLM marker. Just across the road is the picturesque ruin of a cabin, at the approximate site of the old Stone House stage station. Accounts vary as to whether this was also a Pony Express station, but it probably was not, since this seems rather far to the south of where the riders crossed the Antelope Range on the way to Schellbourne. Please remember that this is private property.

Turn right (north) and follow this road as it swings back to the west. After 3.7 miles look for another Pony Express trail marker where we rejoin the trail as it comes in from the right (east). There may have been a station called Spring Valley here, but it seems much too close to Schell Creek. Another 5.3 miles takes you up and over a pass. At the summit, a gray Pony Express marker on the left (just after the cattle guard) indicates where the old Pony Express/stagecoach road descended. The present telephone line traces the approximate route, and the old trail is easily visible here.

It's 2.4 miles down to the site of the old town of Schellbourne on the left. THIS IS NOW A PRIVATE FAMILY RANCH. While the Schellbourne ruins may be of certain archaeological value, they are probably of later date than the Pony Express. The more likely site of Schell Creek Station is another 0.25 mile down the road, at the end of the meadow to the left, beside the creek. There's a marker here indicating where the old trail crossed the present road.

Continue down to the intersection with US 93 and the Schellbourne store/cafe/bar/gas station/motel/RV park. Note the BLM Pony Express interpretive site at the intersection, which gives the distance to the county road for Egan as 0.5 mile south. In fact, the road is directly across the intersection, beside the present Schellbourne station. The actual Pony Express route parallels this road, about 0.5 mile north. Stop in at the cafe to check out their beautiful hand-painted mural/map of the entire Pony Express route.

Some desert roads can be tough on vehicles.

NEVADA TRAVEL INFORMATION

For the Pony Express enthusiast, Nevada largely continues (and intensifies) the remote and rugged qualities of the trail across western Utah. This is desert country, rough, dusty, and arid, all the way to the valley of the Carson River. Of all the country crossed from St. Joseph to Sacramento, this stretch of trail has changed least since the days of the Pony Express.

Nevada has much to offer the tourist. Here the traveler finds some of the most wildly beautiful landscapes in the entire country, the remnants and ruins of wave after wave of mining activity that came and disappeared (if you're into ghost towns, this is the place), and, of course, the famous casino gambling (for adults over twenty-one) and nightlife of its bigger towns. And, yes, the official state flower really is the sagebrush!

Camping at state recreation areas is generally $4 to $5 a night. Always inquire locally about off-highway road conditions, and be sure to carry plenty of water and supplies.

SCHELLBOURNE TO EUREKA

If you don't have a rugged vehicle with high clearance, just forget about the next Pony Byway. Save your pennies, buy yourself a four-wheel-drive vechicle for Christmas, and come back next summer for this drive.

If you do skip Byway #6, drive instead south on US 93, thirty-nine miles to Ely. Note the huge piles of slag from the defunct copper smelter at McGill. This town has a rather unique municipal park and pool that can be a welcome relief on a blistering day. The pool is set within the sea of slag piles, which look like sinister black sand dunes. Since I didn't see any locals with flippers and gills, it might even be ecologically sound.

ELY

(all services)

There's plenty to see in and around Ely. This was, for many years, the center of one of the country's major copper mining areas, and the hills around Ely are full of old gold diggings as well. Ely has a first-rate railroad museum that features steam railroad rides during summer months. Make for the chamber of commerce for a complete list of attractions.

White Pine Chamber of Commerce 636 Aultman St.

Ely is the eastern gateway to the section of US 50 dubbed by *Life Magazine* as "The Loneliest Road in America." The seventy-nine-mile highway drive from here to Eureka is one of the best blacktop desert drives in the country, though considerably south of the Pony Express route.

PONY BYWAY 6: SCHELLBOURNE TO EUREKA

THE FOLLOWING SCHELLBOURNE - EUREKA ROUTE IS FOR HARDCORE PONY EXPRESS ENTHUSIASTS INTENT ON FOLLOWING THE OLD TRAIL IN VEHICLES SUITABLE FOR EXTREMELY ROUGH ROADS. Be advised that the roads from here west vary greatly in condition, and at times the route may be indistinct. In any case, you can expect this drive to be rather rough and slow, but also very beautiful and extremely interesting, with lots of picturesque animal carcasses and bones bleaching in the sun to remind you of the severity of the environment.

Fill up with fuel and water, and give your hoses and tires a good look, because what follows will make Byway #5 seem like highway driving. You will cross several good north-south roads on this drive, most of which can take you south to US 50 if you tire of the wilderness driving.

MAP 13: SCHELLBOURNE TO EUREKA

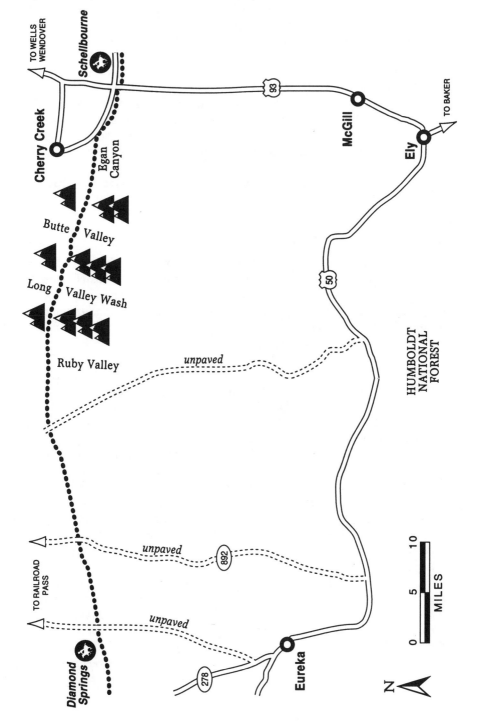

The county road to Egan Canyon is a continuation of the road on which you came into Schellbourne. At mile five, ignore the fork to the left (south) and head due west toward the mountains on excellent road. Nine miles west of US 93 the road angles north at the foot of the hills and deteriorates to decent gravel. About 1.4 miles farther, look for a BLM Pony Express sign, indicating a left (west) turn into the hills.

Egan Canyon was named for Howard Egan, who pioneered this route for Chorpenning's service in the 1850s and who was the Pony Express superintendent for the division from Salt Lake to Robert's Creek. The canyon was on the boundary of the Goshute and Shoshone tribal territories. With it's many thickets and rock outcrops, it's easy to see why this was the site of several Indian ambushes.

Two Pony-era incidents are indicative of how dangerous this spot was at the time.

Egan Canyon Excitement

One of the most colorful stories of Pony Express daring was born when Howard Egan (there is some confusion over whether it was Howard the elder or his son of the same name) came across an Indian camp one dark night, halfway up this canyon. Egan considered turning back and trying to advance by means of another canyon farther to the north, but decided instead to make a bold dash right through the camp.

Egan galloped ahead, yelling and firing his revolver in the air. The Indians must have thought they were under attack by a large party of Whites, and dispersed before him. Once past the camp, Egan would have been confident his fast pony would not be caught from behind. He was later told by a friendly Indian that the local braves had indeed planned to trap a rider, out of curiosity over what he carried that made him ride so fast.

"The Battle of Egan Canyon" is another of those often repeated Pony Express tales that seems to shift in details from source to source. Precise details aside, it seems the station keeper and either a rider or stock tender were attacked one morning in July, 1860 by a large party of Indians. They defended the cabin until their ammunition ran out and they were captured. Instead of killing them right away, the Indians tied them and piled sagebrush around them, intending to burn them alive. At the last moment, the U.S. Cavalry came riding to the rescue—literally.

The eastbound express rider, in approaching the station, had heard the commotion and turned around to gallop back to where he had recently met a party of dragoons who were billeted in Ruby Valley since the start of the Paiute War. The soldiers surprised the Indians, running them off and killing seventeen of them. There is some speculation that three of the graves in the nearby Fort Pearce Cemetery are those of three soldiers reported killed in this battle.

Eastern Nevada.

It was probably the same band of Indians, disappointed at the interruption of their sport, who later that day raided Schell Creek Station, killing three Pony Express employees and driving off all the livestock. Evidently, the Indians also returned to Egan Station in early October. When Burton passed here on October 5, he reported:

> *"Under the circumstances, it was cold comfort to find when we had cleared the kanyon that Egan's Station at the further mouth had been reduced to a chimney stack and a few charred posts. The Gosh-Yutas had set fire to it two or three days before our arrival in revenge for the death of seventeen of their men by Lt. Weed's party. We could distinguish the pits from which the wolves had torn up the corpses, and one fellow's arm projected from the snow."*

The first couple of miles up Egan Canyon are on good road, past lots of interesting old mining sites. Watch for the metal posts with "XP" in white, as well as the familiar gray markers. At mile 2.1 take the right fork, well marked for Butte Valley, Ruby Valley, and the Pony Express Trail. Egan Station was probably just past the left-hand fork, on private land. Just after this fork, note the old Fort Pearce Cemetery on the right.

Eureka, Nevada.

Beyond the cemetery, the route becomes rather rough and indistinct. In fact, there's a maze of dirt roads over Cherry Summit, any of which should get you across, and routing across this whole area is liable to change over the next few years as roads are (hopefully) consolidated and new markers put up. In dry conditions, the road is passable without four-wheel-drive, provided you have decent clearance, but this route may not be practical for any vehicle when wet.

Keep an eye open for Pony Express trail markers, but don't be too worried if you don't see them for some distance because these have a habit of disappearing to souvenir hunters (in fact, the brown stumps of chainsawed BLM trail markers are a good indication you're still on route!). Just keep heading west, and you'll eventually reach Butte Valley, where things will become more obvious.

Two miles or so past the cemetery, you will start to climb up and over Cherry Summit. The road on either side of the summit is the roughest, and you might wish you were on a horse instead of in a vehicle. After about 1.5 miles of descent, you will cross a graded north-south gravel road, and 0.25 mile west of this you will see Butte Valley spread out below.

MAP 14: FT. PEARCE CEMETERY

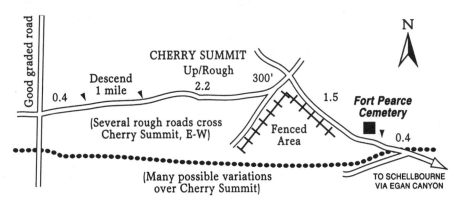

NOTE: The somewhat indistinct route from Fort Pearce Cemetery over Cherry Summit may be consolidated and better marked in the near future.

At first glance, Butte Valley might seem a place only a rattlesnake could love. To be sure, it *is* desolate: a good place for bombing practice (as much of Nevada is used for), or maybe to film the latest Mad Max movie. But these desert landscapes have a real primitive power, and there's definitely something fascinating about a place that's so forbidding to human habitation that it manages to resist change in a rapidly changing world.

Continue west across the valley, about eight miles on smooth, fast road. Climb into the hills at the other side (a Pony Express station was somewhere along here), then drive another eight miles to an obvious deep draw at Long Valley Wash. Just past this wash is a group of road signs (including, in 1993, a Pony Express trail marker that had escaped capture). Continue west four miles to the start of obvious climb, then 1.5 miles up and over.

Mountain Springs Station was probably on the west side of this ridge, possibly near the present stock corral where the road jogs from south to west, or perhaps one mile farther, near the Pony Express marker. Just past this marker, the road descends along what is clearly a seasonal stream, with the obvious track of what might once have been an old wagon/stage trail on the far side.

At the eastern edge of gorgeous Ruby Valley you will come across more Pony Express trail markers. Just keep heading west, on smooth, straight road, toward the ranch (private) visible on the west side of the valley.

Ruby Station sat just southwest of Station Butte, the isolated hill near the west edge of the valley. This had been an old Chorpenning station in 1859, before being rebuilt by the Pony Express. This valley was one of the few places along the trail across central Nevada that was suitable for agriculture. Grain and other foods were grown here on a large scale (as many as one thousand acres were cultivated, including twenty-five acres of potatoes and vegetables) to supply stage and express stations in both directions. During the Paiute War of 1860, a company of U.S. cavalry was sent here from Camp Floyd, where they spent several months patrolling the region. The original Pony Express station was dismantled and moved to Elko, where it can be seen at the Northeastern Nevada Museum.

There is a well-developed BLM campground (drinking water) at Ruby Marsh Recreation Site, about eighteen miles north of here on well-marked roads.

US 50 is twenty-one miles to the south, on the gravel superhighway you will cross to the southwest of the ranch.

To continue along the Pony Express route, drive west 8.3 miles beyond this major north-south road, then take the left fork leading down to Huntington Valley. Cross another graded north-south road, then continue five miles to yet another good north-south road, indicating US 50 forty-two miles south and Elko sixty-nine miles north. Jacob's Wells express station was probably near one of two cattle watering troughs that you'll pass on the right, just before this intersection.

The Express trail west of here is over rough road and private land, so if you wish to continue on to visit the site of Diamond Springs Station, you should turn right (north) here and go over Railroad Pass on excellent road. Otherwise, this is a good place to head for US 50, as this road becomes paved a few miles south of here.

The ruins of Diamond Springs Station are clearly marked to the right (west) of the road, in a cottonwood grove. This is private property, but open to visitors.

Continue south, past the ranch, to the first road on the right (west). It is 11.4 miles of smooth, straight driving across this desert valley, with a few Pony Express markers but no signs. This is one of those places where you will get a real idea of how lonely these rides must have been. Somewhere near the intersection with the good north-south road along the western edge of the valley was the site of Sulphur Springs Station, of which nothing remains.

Not much exists of the old trail and stations (Roberts Creek and Grubb's Well) from here till Dry Creek. Since Dry Creek is easily reached from US 50, it is most expedient to head south to the highway on this good north-south road (ignoring the Pony Express trail marker 1.1 miles south of this intersection). Three miles south of the marker, you will intersect (paved) Nevada 278. A left turn will bring you quickly to US 50 and Eureka.

EUREKA

(most services)

Eureka is a good place to relax and resupply. After the desolation of the drive from Schellbourne, this quiet little outpost on US 50 may seem positively bustling.

EUREKA TO AUSTIN

This is one of the lonelier stretches of "The Loneliest Road in America." For those who chose to do the previous Pony Byway, it will also seem a smooth, fast contrast to primitive desert roads.

Don't miss the very interesting stone carvings called the **Hickison Petroglyphs,** clearly marked, about forty-five miles west of Eureka. There is a pleasant BLM campground here, but it is basic (no drinking water). There's a smaller campground at Scott Summit, about eighteen miles west on US 50, that does have water.

To visit the site of Dry Creek Station, go east from Hickison 1.3 miles on US 50 to a county road to the north. The monument (usual bronze plaque, set in a boulder) and some stone foundations are on private property about 300 yards to the left (west) of the road. They can't quite be seen from the road, but if you continue on up to the ranch, you should find someone who can tell you which gate to enter. As more folks request directions, the owners may be prompted to put up a sign on the road—provided visitors remember to close the gate behind them.

Dry Creek was one of the stations destroyed during the Paiute uprising of May, 1860. This was also where, according to one long-standing (and sometimes debated) legend, a rider came in severely wounded, fell from his saddle and died. Similar stories are told of other Nevada stations, and they probably all relate to the same incident.

One incident of the Paiute War that does appear to have taken place here occurred in late May, 1860.

Rough Day at Dry Creek Station

Ralph Rosier, the station keeper, and a stock tender named Applegate were busy one morning preparing breakfast. As Rosier was going to the spring for water, he was shot dead by a Paiute war party. When Applegate ran to help his friend, he too was shot but made it back to the station.

Si McCandless, a trader who kept a store across from the station, ran to the station, where he joined the critically wounded Applegate and another express employee named Bolwinkle. McCandless and Bolwinkle frantically stacked grain sacks in the doorway and loaded weapons, while Applegate pleaded for them to leave him and make a run for it. Applegate then asked for a pistol, which he promptly used to blow his own brains out.

The Paiutes did not immediately attack the station, seeming content to sit and wait. Meanwhile, McCandless convinced Bolwinkle that their best

MAP 15: EUREKA TO COLD SPRINGS

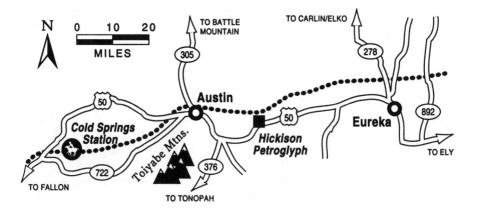

chance was to abandon the station to the Indians and run for the next station. McCandless felt that all the Indians really wanted was to plunder the station, and that his own reputation for fairness among the local tribes might grant them some safety.

The two lit out on foot, without serious pursuit from the Indians, who did, indeed, make busy pillaging. For some reason, Bolwinkle took off in his stocking feet, and when they reached the next station, after a run of twelve miles, his feet were a mess.

Prior to Austin's development in the early 1860s, the stage and Pony routes through the Toiyabe range west of here ran farther to the north than the present highway.

AUSTIN

(most services—very few motel rooms, and possibly the most expensive fuel prices in America)

Austin didn't really develop until 1862-1863, after a former express rider discovered silver here and started a fifty million dollar mining rush. By the middle 1860s there were ten thousand people in and around the new town. Prior to this the Pony Express and Central Overland Stage kept a station at Jacobsville, on the Reese River west of Austin and just north of present-day US 50. With Austin's rise, Jacobsville dwindled and eventually died.

It must have been an exciting place back then, with miners and speculators in a wild money frenzy. One of the more "creative" stock promotion scams in the history of western mining took place with the formation of the Reese River Navigation Company, ostensibly for the purpose of transporting ore by barge from the Austin area ninety-two miles north to Battle Mountain. Since the Reese River is a piddling little creek that for most of the year will barely float an inner tube, its promoters must have had either tremendous optimism or tremendous sense of humor.

Today Austin is a sleepy, friendly little place that somehow seems much larger than it really is, after driving across so many miles of desert wasteland. There isn't a lot to see here. A handful of nineteenth century buildings hint at a mining heyday that's long since passed. This isn't quite a ghost town, but it seems to hover perilously close. Of the several mining-era buildings left in town, most interesting is the famous **International Hotel,** which was disassembled and moved piece by piece from Virginia City in 1863. It serves as Austin's premier eatery and saloon. Look for it on the right, near the west (lower) end of Main Street.

Stokes Castle sits high on a ridge southwest of town. A replica of a medieval Italian tower, it was built by a mining and railroad magnate as a summer family home. It's pretty uninspiring, as castles go, and it's fenced off from public entry, but the views from here are definitely worth the five-minute drive. If you look off to the north and west, you can see where the Pony trail cut across the Reese River toward the old Jacobsville townsite. From Austin, turn left (south) on Castle Road, just below the Chevron gas station.

Stokes Castle, Austin, Nevada.

Sidetrip From Austin: Toiyabe National Forest

Austin is the gateway to terrific outdoor activities in the Toiyabe National Forest, south of town. The USDA Forest Service maintains a helpful information desk at their Austin office, where you can pick up useful material on camping and attractions. The office is just west of town, on the right, just before the intersection with Nevada 305, which runs north to Battle Mountain.

Highlights of a half-day excursion from Austin might include:

Twenty-one miles southeast of Austin (on Monitor Valley Road) is the very informal spa called **Spencer Hot Springs.** The 140-degree Fahrenheit mineral spring flows into a simple concrete tub, with remnants of wooden tubs used by early settlers nearby. There are no amenities here and no cold water.

Nine miles beyond the hot springs is **Toquima Cave,** where you can see Indian pictographs. This is also a good place to watch eagles. There is primitive camping here, but no water. Park at Pete's Summit and hike 0.25 mile to the cave.

Diana's Punch Bowl is a large hot spring, about seventy-five feet in diameter. The spring is not fenced, so be careful, especially with small children.

Travelers have a choice of two highways to follow from Austin to Cold Springs. The most direct route is to stay on US 50 over New Pass Summit, approximately fifty miles to the Cold Springs interpretive site. Alternately, the old highway (now Nevada 722), which branches south from US 50 two miles west of Austin, is an extremely attractive drive, with great views from Railroad Pass. The actual line of the Pony Express ran between these two routes.

It used to be possible to visit the site of Smith Creek Station, and drive over the Desatoya Mountains to Cold Springs. Unfortunately, the present owner of this private land has decided to lock his gate to through traffic. Perhaps this situation will be changed in the future to allow Pony Express travelers to drive this attractive stretch of trail, but until then it is prudent to stick to one of the highways.

If you choose the Nevada 722 route, you will have to backtrack ten miles east on US 50, where it rejoins Nevada 722, in order to visit Cold Springs. If you drive US 50, stop at the prominent BLM interpretive site for the telegraph and stage station at New Pass.

There are extensive ruins and a BLM interpretive site at **Cold Springs.** The ruins alongside the highway are from the later stagecoach station. To visit the actual Pony Express site requires a 1.5-mile hike (well marked from the BLM site), but it is well worth it. This is one of the best archaeological sites of the entire Pony Express trail, and should not be missed. Among the 55-foot by 135-foot stone ruin, it is easy to discern the corrals and living quarters, as well as several gunports in the two-foot-thick walls.

Cold Springs was attacked several times by Indians during the Paiute War of 1860. When Bob Haslam made his famous ride from Fridays Station (Lake Tahoe) to Smith Creek, he made his final change of horses here. The following morning, on his return ride west, he found the stationkeeper dead and the station in ruins.

One mile northeast of the site, on US 50, is a cafe/gas station that appears to be open in the daytime only.

The Paiute War and Pony Bob's Long Ride

This part of Nevada was the heart of a bitter war between settlers and native Paiutes in 1860. In early May, 1860, Williams Station (ten miles northwest of later Fort Churchill) was destroyed and five men killed. There were corresponding attacks on neighboring ranches and other stations.

Older Paiute chiefs pleaded for peace, but the younger braves were hot for war. Anticipating further hostilities, prospectors and ranchers from throughout northwest Nevada gathered at Carson City and Virginia City for protection.

A militia party of 105 men assembled at Carson City, then marched north toward Pyramid Lake, intent on punishing the Indians. The over-confident volunteers were led into a clever ambush and routed, with nearly half of their force killed, including their commander.

A force of federal troops pursued the Indians, but the Paiute band simply dissolved into the wilderness they knew so well. Smaller bands of Indians roamed the wilderness trails across central Nevada, raiding stage and express stations and harassing the riders.

"Pony Bob" Haslam left Friday's Station, near the south shore of Lake Tahoe in late May, on his run to Buckland's Station, fifty miles to the east. At Buckland's, Haslam's relief rider refused to ride, due to the recent outbreak of hostilities. Haslam agreed to continue on to the next home station, at Smith Creek, another 107 miles. His ride east was long, exhausting, and nerve-wracking, but uneventful.

After a short rest at Smith Creek, the mochila from the east came in, so Bob mounted up to ride it back to Friday's. At Cold Springs, where he had changed horses just the evening before, he found the station in ruins and the keeper dead. At Sand Springs he convinced the lone stock tender to ride with him west to the relative security of Carson Sink Station. At Carson Sink they found a small group gathered for mutual defense, so Bob left his companion and continued west to Bucklands, and eventually all the way back to Friday's. He had ridden more than 320 miles, across some of the roughest country of the entire trail, during the single most dangerous period in Pony Express history.

By the end of May, 1860 most of the stations between Carson Sink and Roberts Creek were either burned or abandoned. Seven stations were destroyed, sixteen men killed (mostly station keepers and stock tenders), and 150 horses lost. Mail service stopped for a month and was intermittent through the summer. These events prompted the building of Fort Churchill for the protection of lands east of the Carson Valley.

SAND MOUNTAIN RECREATION AREA
(no services/no water)

Thirty-four miles west of Cold Springs is one of the more interesting geological formations you'll see anywhere, along with one of the best Pony Express archaeological sites of the entire trail.

Sand Mountain is a single, immense sand dune that rises out of the surrounding brush-covered alkali desert. It is clearly seen from the highway, just a mile or so to the north.

To visit the extensive ruins of **Sand Springs Station,** turn right (north) 0.5 mile past the sign for "loneliest phone." Take the left at the prominent fork and drive to the parking area. The right fork continues to the recreation area, where there are rough campsites but NO WATER.

Looking at Sand Springs Station you get an idea of just how desperate early pioneers in this wasteland were for anything that even resembled decent water. This was no doubt the best they could do, yet the water at

Ruins of Sand Springs Station.

MAP 16: SAND MOUNTAIN TO LAKE TAHOE

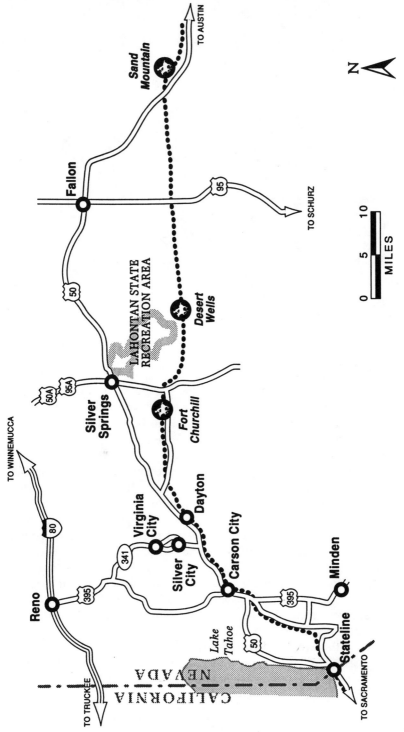

Four wheelers at Sand Mountain Recreation Area.

this place was described as warm and smelly, with a taste equal to rinsing a mail rider's socks.

From Sand Springs, the Pony trail ran northeast of modern US 50 for a few miles, then cut straight west across the dry bed of Carson Lake. The actual Pony Express route is difficult to trace and crosses private property, so the best driving route is via Fallon on US 50.

This is as "desert" as it gets, and anyone who crossed this wasteland in the 1860s was an adventurer of heroic proportion. Two miles west of the turnoff for Sand Mountain, about 100 feet off to the right of US 50, sits the gravesite of four young children who didn't make it, victims of diphtheria during a wagon crossing in 1864. This gravesite is worth stopping to see, as it is an excellent example of a quirky sort of folk-art memorial. The artist who created the site has written the story of the discovery of the original grave, and adorned the present site with all manner of bric-a-brac. What's even more interesting and more poignant is the odd assortment of casual mementoes left by passersby. To the left of this site, note the stumps of the old telegraph line. This is the approximate course of the actual Pony Express route.

Sixteen miles west of Sand Mountain is **Grimes Point Prehistoric Rock Art Site.** Unlike Eureka, Austin, or Fallon, this is one place in central Nevada where there were people living before the Pony Express rode by—as much as *8,000 years* before.

Here, on the banks of an ancient lake, stone-age hunters recorded incidents of their kills, from a time when animals thrived in the lush wetlands that disappeared long ago. It is fascinating to imagine the amount of life this now-sterile basin once supported. A bit over a mile north, along the well-marked dirt road, is **Hidden Cave Interpretive Site.** Both interpretive trails are self-guided, and definitely worth seeing.

FALLON

(all services, camping at nearby Lahontan State Park.)

Fallon didn't exist even at the turn of the century. The town owes its birth to water projects initiated around 1903, and its growth to the building of nearby Lahontan Dam between 1911 and 1915. After the landscapes of the past couple hundred miles, it should be no surprise that a place with water would be a big hit in this part of the world.

After a couple of days in the desert, driving into Fallon is like entering paradise—a cool, green paradise. With its groves of trees, gardens, and fields of green grass and alfalfa, Fallon is like an emerald isle in the midst of a sea of sun-baked sand and sagebrush. No wonder the town bills itself "The Oasis of Nevada."

It's amazing how a little roughing it can color one's impression. Fallon has all those creature comforts you've somehow managed to live without the past couple of days: a real strip with drive-ins and lots of motels; real, full-sized, twenty-four-hour supermarkets; a real selection on the radio (and the first National Public Radio reception since the Salt Lake Valley); and real casinos, too. And trees. Remember those things? Fallon appears to be experiencing a mini-boom as one of the few places in this region that's fit for human habitation.

US 50 becomes Williams Avenue, Fallon's main east-west street. Notice the prominent **Churchill County Courthouse** on the right, at the intersection with Fallon's main north-south thoroughfare, Maine Street (yes, that's Maine, with an E, after the home state of Fallon's founder). Turn left here to visit the excellent **Churchill County Museum,** and to follow the Pony Express trail to Fort Churchill.

The Churchill County Museum is a must stop for anyone interested in the settlement of one of America's greatest wildernesses. There are exhibits of material from Hidden Cave, of later Native American life, and of the pioneer period of central Nevada that somehow seems not so far back in the past.

So what the heck is the Navy doing in the middle of the Nevada desert, anyway? Training carrier-based aviators, is what. Fallon is home to the actual, genuine Navy "Top-Gun" flight school, officially called the **Naval Strike Warfare College.** The Fallon Air Station boasts the longest U.S. Navy runway in the world: 14,000 feet. They hold their air show in October.

MAP 17: FALLON TO FORT CHURCHILL

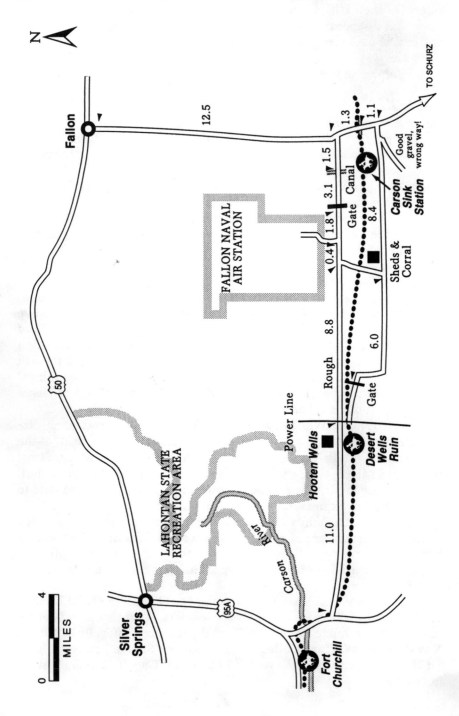

N

MILES
0   4

Fallon

12.5

FALLON NAVAL AIR STATION

LAHONTAN STATE RECREATION AREA

50

Silver Springs

95A

Carson River

Power Line

Hooten Wells

Rough 8.8

11.0

6.0

Gate

Desert Wells Ruin

Gate Canal

Sheds & Corral

8.4

3.1   1.5

1.8

0.4

Carson Sink Station

1.3

1.1

TO SCHURZ

Good gravel, wrong way!

Fort Churchill

If you happen to be near Fallon around the third week of July, don't miss the annual All-Indian Rodeo and Stampede, with its parade and powwow.

I: Churchill County Museum, 1050 South Maine Street, (702) 423-3677.

From Fallon, it is possible to rejoin the old Pony Express trail across to Fort Churchill, on what is an extremely attractive and interesting desert drive. The route described below is on good dirt road, passable by all vehicles (except perhaps the largest RVs) in dry conditions. One might also save an hour or so by sticking to US 50, west to Silver Springs, then south on Alternate US 95 to Fort Churchill.

PONY BYWAY 7: FALLON TO FORT CHURCHILL

From the Churchill County Museum continue south on Maine Street, which becomes US 95. Of the two routes shown on the map, the southern road is smoother, while the northern is a few miles shorter and possibly slightly closer to the actual Pony trail. The northern road is mostly fine, but rough in spots, and probably impassable for conventional vehicles when wet. The southern road is excellent, fast gravel that stays well above the flats to the immediate north that can be treacherously slick.

CARSON SINK STATION:

Carson Sink Station got its name from the way nearby Carson Lake just disappears, or "sinks" into the desert. Because there are no trees or rocks here, the Pony Express station was built of adobe, a kind of hardened mud. Unfortunately, adobe eventually melts under precipitation, so only a trace remains of the original structure.

The site and marker for Carson Sink Station are probably not worth the effort it takes to find them, under the present obscure conditions. You can get a good idea of what the place must have been like simply by looking due west along the south side of the prominent irrigation canal. If you insist, drive west on a faint track (FOUR-WHEEL-DRIVE ONLY!) along the south side of the canal for about 0.5 mile, until you notice a slight trend to the left (south). Climb on top of your vehicle and look to the south for a low yellow marker, then walk to the site. If you encounter even the slightest wetness along the way, don't challenge it. This soil type can be incredibly slick when wet, and it's just not worth it. If you're still adamant about finding the station site, and if you have a suitable four-wheel-drive vehicle, you might head south (left) for the north edge of the drier alkali flat, then make your own way west. Park near the prominent wooden post—do not attempt to drive north. Walk thirty to forty yards northeast from the post, and look for the low yellow marker and the faint outline of the eroded adobe walls that have nearly disappeared. Now, aren't you proud of yourself for going to all that trouble?

Wall mural.

CARSON SINK TO DESERT WELLS

Just before US 95 begins its climb out of the alkali flats of Carson Sink, note the well-maintained (but unmarked as yet) gravel road to the right (west). Opposite this road, on the left (east) side of US 95, is a large wooden sign with "Entering Newlands Irrigation Project" on its southern side.

Turn right (west). Immediately after leaving US 95, take the unmarked dirt road on the right. Do not stay on the good gravel road, as it turns very rough after a few miles. Stay on this quite good dirt road, ignoring all side tracks. After 8.4 miles you will encounter an attractive cluster of ranch sheds and corrals. The road continues west, then arcs north along a line of hills to the west. Six miles beyond the sheds take the obvious left (west) through an open gate up and over the hills. Descend past a prominent pond, then cross beneath a huge power line (hear it crackle?!). It is less than a mile to the ruins of Hooten Well.

This corral, trough, and ruined shack, picturesque as they may be, are not the ruins of Desert Wells Pony Express Station. To find the station site, drive or walk south along the east side of the north-south fence, 1.2 miles. The track is fair, but you might prefer walking to bouncing your family sedan over it. The ruins are fairly obvious, on the left (east) of the track. This station was probably used only during the last months of the Pony Express, when it also served as a telegraph station. As always in this country, WATCH FOR SNAKES!

Continue eleven miles west down the valley, on the obvious main road, avoiding all spurs. When you reach the highway (Alternate US 95), turn right (north) and cross the Carson River. On the right is the site of old Bucklands Station. The present wooden building dates from about 1870. Another 0.6 mile north is the well-marked turnoff on the left for Fort Churchill.

FORT CHURCHILL STATE HISTORIC PARK

(camping, water)

Fort Churchill was built in response to the Pyramid Lake (Paiute) Indian War of 1860. It replaced nearby Buckland's as the stage and Pony Express station, with the fort headquarters as stopping point for the mail riders. The post was abandoned in 1869 and sat vacant until 1957 when it became a state historic park. Rather than restoring the buildings to period condition, they have merely been stabilized (the adobe treated with waterproofing to prevent further disintegration) and thus kept in a very photogenic state of semi-decay. Begin your visit at the interpretive center, then take some time to wander about the extensive ruins.

There is a pleasant basic campground here, in a shady grove beside the Carson River.

Fort Churchill State Historic Park.

CHAPTER SEVEN

OUT OF THE WILDERNESS: FORT CHURCHILL, NEVADA, TO SACRAMENTO, CALIFORNIA

My informants declared that in and about Carson a dead man for breakfast was the rule; besides accidents perpetually occurring to indifferent or to peace-making parties, they reckoned per annum fifty murders. In a peculiar fit of liveliness an intoxicated gentleman will discharge his revolver in a ball-room, and when a "shyooting" begins in the thin walled frame houses, those not concerned avoid bullets and splinters by jumping into their beds. During my three days' stay at Carson City I heard of three murders.

—Burton, p. 552

From Fort Churchill west, this is no longer a wilderness trail. In fact, the Sacramento to Carson City run was a fairly civilized (albeit rugged) ride, even in 1860-1861. Today this is largely a string of resort communities, strip developments, and suburbs. The important thing to remember here is to shift touristic gears, from the adventuresome wilderness driving of the Utah and Nevada deserts to the more "citified" pleasures of Carson City, Tahoe, and Sacramento, and the now very peaceful remnants of the old Forty-Niner mining districts in the California hills.

FORT CHURCHILL TO DAYTON

From Fort Churchill you can continue north on Alternate U.S. Highway 95 to rejoin US 50, or do the scenic sixteen-mile drive on good gravel road (suitable for all vehicles) along the Carson River.

Approximate Pony Express route in the Carson River Valley.

West of Fort Churchill the landscape changes considerably. Driving along the verdant Carson River it becomes clear that Bob Haslam had one of the choicest sections of the trail. No longer bleak desert, the terrain is once again shifting toward alpine. Cows graze in the lush river bottom, though there is plenty of sagebrush to remind us that this is still Nevada. About thirteen miles west of Fort Churchill there was a Pony Express station along the Carson River called, variously, Miller's or Reed's. Nothing remains of this station.

At mile 14.8 look for a Pony Express marker just before a fork in the road. Take the left fork (marked River Road) 1.4 miles to a left turn on Cardelli Road. Another 2.4 miles brings you to US 50, just at the outskirts of Dayton. Turn left to drive into town.

DAYTON
(most services)

Dayton began as a convenient campground on the Carson River for desert-weary emigrants in the California rush of 1849-1850. When gold was discovered in a nearby canyon to the northwest, Dayton grew as a supply center for the diggings. The later silver strikes on the Comstock Lode caused Dayton to blossom into one of the prettiest and most substantial communities in the region. Take a few minutes to poke around the pleasantly non-touristic old town center.

The first Pony Express station in Dayton was called Spafford's Hall, now a gravel pit. The second station was at the present site of the Union Hotel.

Sidetrip: Virginia City

Just west of Dayton is the turnoff to the right for Virginia City and Gold Hill, seven miles north on Nevada Highway 341. This is really a must-see sidetrip; it would be a shame to miss what is probably the best, touristic old mining town in the nation.

Virginia City began as a tent and lean-to mining camp after gold was discovered here in 1859. For the early gold miners, the biggest problem was the sticky bluish-gray muck that clogged their sluice boxes and hindered their shoveling. That muck turned out to be very rich silver ore, and the rush to the new Comstock Lode was on. The roads across the Sierra Nevada were crowded with a steady stream of hopeful miners vacating the dwindling, ten-year-old California gold-rush towns.

At the height of the Comstock silver rush, as many as 25,000 people lived in Virginia City. The mineral wealth of this district (reputedly over $400 million in silver and gold) helped finance the Union war effort, and the rush to the Comstock was largely responsible for the population growth that allowed Nevada's early (1864) statehood.

In its heyday, Virginia City was probably the richest town in the world, in terms of per capita production. It had four banks, six churches, five police precincts, a substantial Chinatown, and a very busy red-light district. Virginia City's International Hotel (yes, the same one you saw in Austin) had the first elevator in the West.

This is where a hard-rock miner named George Hearst literally struck it rich, establishing the great Hearst family fortune. This was also where a young reporter named Sam Clemens established a reputation as a writer of some ability. These are perhaps the two most famous names of a long list of fascinating characters who helped build Virginia City's legend as "Queen of the Comstock."

Today the town is a lively combination of nineteenth-century living-history museum and Victorian-era theme park, where people of all ages and interests will surely find much to enthuse over. There are train rides on the historic Virginia & Truckee Railroad (considered one of the richest and most famous of all short-line railroads), underground mine tours, fine old commercial buildings and beautiful mansions, several museums (one devoted to the illicit activities of Virginia City's notorious "entertainment district"), lively saloons with plenty of period entertainment and, of course, legal gambling.

CARSON CITY

(all services)

Abram Curry founded the future capital of Nevada in 1858, through an act of stubbornness. Curry had tried in vain to secure a decent building lot for a fair price in the old Mormon settlement at Genoa. Infuriated by what he felt was unfair pricing, Curry bought a settler's ranch a little farther up the valley and laid out his own townsite. The following year began the Comstock silver rush, and Carson City boomed.

Today Carson City is one of the smallest and most laid-back state capitals in the country. It's easy to get around and a good place to catch up on all those post office/library/laundry/car service chores, but there isn't a lot to see and do here.

The Carson Pony Express station was on Carson Street (the main north-south thoroughfare, also US 395), between 4th and 5th streets, approximately across from the present Legislative Building. The **Nevada State Museum,** at 600 N. Carson Street, was originally built as a United States mint and served in that capacity until 1933. Today it houses excellent exhibits on the anthropology, mining, and archaeology of Nevada and the Desert West. The museum is open daily, 8:30 a.m. to 4:30 p.m. Admission is $1.50 for adults.

The **Nevada State Railroad Museum** is south of town at 2180 South Carson Street. There's a fine collection of equipment (five steam locomotives and several restored coaches) and photographs from the Vir-

Casino glitter of Carson City.

ginia & Truckee Railroad, which operated from the late 1860s until 1950. Train rides are available Wednesday through Sunday, 8:30 a.m. to 4:30 p.m., May 23 through November 2. Admission is $1 for adults, kids are free.

There's a large, convenient (but showerless) state park campground at Washoe Lake, which is four miles north on US 395, then right at a well-marked turn. Finally, Don't forget to take advantage of the excellent casino buffets while in Carson City.

CARSON TO STATELINE

Three miles south of Carson, continue south on US 395, ignoring the turnoff for US 50 on the right. A mile or so farther, take the well-marked turnoff on the right for Jack's Valley Road (Nevada 206). Just after Jack's Valley School (note the Pony Express marker across from school), this road turns due south and runs nine miles to Genoa.

Genoa is a pretty little place, with a restaurant, cafe, and general store. The site of the Pony Express livery station is now a pleasant picnic area, next to the restored stockade at **Mormon Station State Historic Park.** The park is open daily, 10:00 a.m. to 4:30 p.m., from mid-May through October. Across the street is the Genoa Courthouse Museum (same hours).

Follow Genoa's main street south, marked for "Kingsbury Grade." Walley's Hot Springs is about two miles south of Genoa. An elegant spa and hotel has occupied this site since 1862. Over the years it has been visited by such luminaries as Mark Twain, President Ulysses S. Grant, and Clark Gable. Today there are six mineral pools, a fresh-water swimming pool, steam and dry sauna rooms, weight rooms, and tennis courts. There are also limited bed-and-breakfast accommodations in attractive cottages, and a lounge. Cost of day use (all day) is $12 per person (sorry, no kids under twelve in the spa area). For information or reservations call (702) 782-8155.

A mile or so past Walley's is the marker for the original Kingsbury Grade Road—the actual route of the Pony Express over Dagget Pass— which is now closed. Six miles south of Genoa take the turnoff for Nevada 207 (Kingsbury/Tahoe), on the right, and climb eight miles to 7,300-foot Dagget Summit. This road is excellent, with gorgeous views out over the Carson Valley, but RVs and vehicles in poor tune may wheeze a bit toward the top.

This might seem more like a mountain wilderness, were it not for all the multi-million-dollar condo developments. One can only imagine how spectacular this must have been just thirty or forty years ago, before the developers transformed it into an alpine subdivision. Oh well, such is private ownership of land in America.

A mile or so down from the summit, beautiful Lake Tahoe comes into view, along with the sprawl of resorts and pricey homes that's sprung up around it. Three miles below the summit, the road rejoins US 50. Turn left, and prepare for major culture shock.

STATELINE/SOUTH LAKE TAHOE

(all services)

These two towns sit side by side on the Nevada/California state line—you'll know you've crossed into California by the sudden absence of casinos. This is a major tourist mecca of mammoth proportion and tremendous variety, a place where pine trees and pickup trucks meet neon lights and Porsches. The town of Stateline is lost in the glitter of a generally characterless entertainment strip. All the major casinos are here for your amusement.

Evidently there really is a big, beautiful lake, along with boat docks, bicycling and hiking trails, and other such outdoorsy attractions, lurking somewhere just beyond the glitter and flash of the casinos. The lake itself really is spectacular, generally considered one of the most beautiful high alpine lakes in the world. There are all sorts of boat tours, dinner cruises, and the like, but it's pretty clear that gambling and nightclub entertainment are the real draw here, at least in town.

The Pony Express riders actually did gallop down the main strip here (some say the route ran behind the present Harrah's), but they were

Pony Express statue outside Harrah's, Stateline.

probably way too busy to stop to pull on a slot machine or take in a show. Friday's Station, Bob Haslam's home station, is now on private property (across from the golf course), with no public access. Harrah's has a great Pony Express statue in front, and a restaurant named for Friday's Station.

With so much going on in and around town, the best bet is to call the Lake Tahoe Visitors Authority for information on activities and attractions. There is also a very informative USDA Forest Service visitor center, offering lots of free maps, brochures, and wilderness hiking information. The center runs several interpretive programs and has six fascinating self-guided trails. To reach the center, from the Pony Express statue at Harrah's, drive 5.1 miles west to the major intersection of US 50 and Emerald Bay Road (California 89) and turn right (north). Camp Richardson (camping here) is about two miles north. One mile beyond is the visitor center, which is open daily, 8 a.m. to 5:30 p.m.

Continue north on California 89 for spectacular views of the lake, Forest Service campgrounds, and for the Tour de Tahoe sidetrip described below.

A special note on overnighting in the Stateline/South Lake Tahoe area is in order: Try to avoid being here on weekends in the summer tourist season unless you have made advance reservations for rooms or camping; competition for both can be fierce.

I: Lake Tahoe Visitors Authority, 1 800 AT-TAHOE (lodging); (916) 544-5050 (attractions).

MAP 18: MEYERS TO WOODFORD

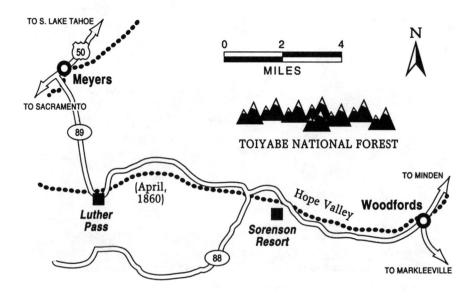

Sidetrip Drive: Seventy-Two-Mile Tour of Lake Tahoe

This is called "The Most Beautiful Drive in America" and it just might be. In addition to the spectacular natural scenery, there are several entertaining man-made attractions to visit along this circular tour. The Lake Tahoe Visitors Authority has a concise but detailed brochure devoted entirely to this drive; the brochure is found on every information board in the area, including the Forest Service visitor center, which is perhaps the most convenient starting point for the tour.

From the visitor center, continue north on California 89 to Tahoe City, then on around the north end of the lake on California 28. Cross the Nevada state line (now on Nevada 28), and run south to rejoin US 50 about fourteen miles northeast of Stateline.

This drive also provides an opportunity to visit the Ponderosa Ranch, made famous by the celebrated television show, Bonanza. Located near Incline Village, on Nevada 28, Ponderosa Ranch offers visitors an entire recreated western town, along with the Cartwright ranch house. The ranch is open from Memorial Day through Labor Day, 9:30 a.m. to 5 p.m. Special morning hay wagon rides and wagon camp breakfasts are offered daily, 8 a.m. to 9:30 a.m.

From present-day South Lake Tahoe/Stateline, the Pony trail ran more or less along the course of US 50, all the way to Sacramento.

From the intersection of US 50 and California 89, continue west on US 50 four miles to the town of Meyers, originally the site of Yank's Station. Look for Yank's Motel on the south side of the road (just before the golf course), where you will find a detailed historical marker. The original station (long gone) was founded as a trading post in the 1850s. It served as a hostelry and stage stop, and as a Pony Express remount station.

From Meyers, there are opportunities for two short Pony-related sidetrips.

Sidetrip to Woodford's, Through Hope Valley

For the first three weeks of service, the Pony Express route ran between Genoa and Strawberry Valley by way of Woodford's Station and Hope Valley, rather than via Friday's Station. This was probably due to the heavy spring snows over the Kingsbury Grade. The drive to Woodford's gives a very good idea of just how attractive the country around Lake Tahoe really is, as soon as you get away from all the traffic and development.

Half a mile west of the site of Yank's Station is the turnoff south for Markleeville. Drive 11.3 pretty miles to a left (east) turn on California 88, then 5.7 even prettier miles, past the attractive cluster of cabins at Sorenson's, to a left turn at the sign "Old Pony Express Trail." Here you will find Woodford's General Store (gas and cafe), with its several Pony Express monuments. Nearby Woodford's Inn has accommodations, and there is camping close by.

Return to US 50 by retracing this drive. Note that Sorenson's, while not exactly budget accommodations, is a very nice place to overnight, perhaps a welcome splurge at the end of a what has been a long and sometimes tiring drive. The cabins (most with kitchens) vary greatly in size and style; they sleep from two to six people, and rent for between $60 and $150 per night, slightly higher on weekends and in winter. Reservations are advised, and if you call (1 800 423-9949 or 916-694-2203) they'll send a detailed brochure describing each cabin.

Sidetrip Hike Along the Pony Express Trail

The 1.5 mile Hawley Grade National Recreational Trail provides an opportunity for car-weary Pony Express enthusiasts to get out and stretch their legs along moderate terrain to Johnson Pass, the actual route used by the riders. From US 50 in Meyers, drive four miles south on Upper Truckee Road (on the left, just past California 89) to Bridge Summer Home Tract and watch for the Hawley Grade sign. The topographic map for this area is the Fallen Leaf quadrangle (available at the USDA Forest Service visitor center back at Lake Tahoe).

Return to US 50 and continue west over Echo Pass and down through dramatic country, past Twin Bridges and popular trailheads into the Desolation Wilderness (with excellent day hiking and backpacking).

About thirteen miles west of Meyers/Yank's, just past the sheer rock cliffs called Lover's Leap (there's a basic campsite here), is attractive Strawberry Lodge. This was the site of Strawberry Valley Station. Lodge manager Richard Mitchell is extremely knowledgeable about local history and has an extensive file of documents and photographs relating to the early days of this historically important stopping place.

Strawberry Lodge offers trail rides and day hikes, and serves as a great base for rock climbing at Lover's Leap, which towers above the lodge. Their thirty-eight double rooms range from $45 to $75, and they also have a restaurant and bar (both popular with climbers and hikers staying in the campsite up the road). Definitely call for room reservations during the summer, at (916) 659-7200. There is also a gas station/convenience store here.

It is nine miles to Kyburz (most services). At the Kyburz fire station (0.8 mile west of town on US 50, on the right) is a marker for the stage and Pony Express station called Sugarloaf House. Continuing down the valley on US 50, drive another 8.5 miles to the marker for Moore's Station, on the right. Shortly after the site of Moore's, US 50 becomes a divided highway for the rest of the journey.

POLLOCK PINES

(most services)

The main street of this peaceful, woodsy town is now called Pony Express Trail, and half the businesses in town seem to be named for the Pony Express. The Pony riders trotted right through the townsite, though the riders probably didn't even slow down to kick at the dogs and stray children who ran out to cheer them along their way.

Though the present restaurant at Sportsmans Hall is not the original, it does occupy approximately the same site as the famous old stage and express station. The decor of this eatery is tied closely to the Pony Express, and there are many Pony-related maps and photos on display. The food is very good, and the place is especially noted for its breakfasts. Sportsmans Hall is located 0.35 mile east of the Cedar Grove exit of US 50 (three miles west of the Pollock Pines exit), or just drive three miles southwest on Pony Express Trail through Pollock Pines.

Return to US 50 and continue ten miles west to Placerville, site of the next station.

PLACERVILLE

(most services)

There is so much to see and do in and around historic Placerville that the tourist information office is a worthwhile first stop. Take the Mosquito Road/Central Placerville exit, turn left under the highway, then right (downhill) on Main Street. The tourist office is on the left, in a pretty, ivy-covered building across from Town Hall. It's hours are Monday through Friday, 8 a.m. to 5 p.m.; Saturday, Sunday, and holidays 10 a.m. to 4 p.m.

MAP 19: PLACERVILLE TO SACRAMENTO

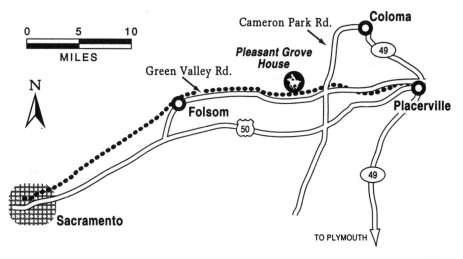

Find a place to park, then spend some time strolling through Placerville's picturesque downtown. The Pony Express stables were on Cary Street, close to where the marker now stands.

There are two fascinating free museums in Placerville, one practically next door to the information office. The larger of the two is the El Dorado County Historical Museum, at 100 Placerville Drive (next to the fairgrounds). They have a very helpful staff and a great selection of souvenirs and books. Hours are Wednesday through Saturday, 10 a.m. to 4 p.m.; Sunday, noon to 4 p.m.

Placerville's Gold Bug Mine is a sixty-one-acre park with over 200 old mines. It is one mile north of Main Street, at Bedford Avenue.

Placerville is also the ideal base for exploring California's Gold Rush Country, spread out along aptly-named California 49 to the north and south of Placerville. Detailed travel information on Gold Country drives is available at the Placerville information office.

Sidetrip Drive: Gold Rush Country

In early January of 1848 a carpenter from New Jersey named James Marshall was sent by his Sacramento employer to build a sawmill on the American River. On the morning of January 24, Marshall was inspecting the mill race when he noticed some flecks of gold in the water. Two months later a San Francisco paper announced the discovery and sparked the largest gold rush the world had yet seen. By late summer, 4,000 miners were crowded into the area, and word of the strike had reached the East.

Forty thousand prospectors arrived in California by sea in 1849. An equal number came overland by wagon train. Though the rush peaked in 1852, emigration continued for several years, until other mineral strikes to the east drew attention away. During the second half of the nineteenth century, 125 million ounces of gold were taken from the hills of California.

Today, California Highway 49, named for the gold rush of that year and running north-south through the foothills of the Sierras, provides a veritable driving tour through the heart of the original gold rush country. The highest concentration of attractions extends between Coloma, eight miles to the north of Placerville, to Columbia State Historic Park, seventy miles south.

COLOMA/MARSHALL GOLD DISCOVERY STATE PARK

Coloma may rightfully claim to be where the wildness of the Wild West actually began. It has been estimated that at one time there were as many as 20,000 people in the area around present-day Coloma, but the strike soon played out and the prospectors drifted off to more promising sites. Very little is left today, and the park is more a memorial to the scene of a historic event than the site of significant archaeological findings.

The old mill has been rebuilt to original specifications, using hand-hewn beams and mortise-and-tenon joints. Marshall's cabin has been preserved, along with several stone buildings. There is a small museum, an impressive monument to Marshall and the rush for gold his discovery provoked, a quiet park, and a campground where one can fish for trout or pan for gold. Buildings are open 10 a.m. to 5 p.m. daily, all year.

A quiet, peaceful place for most of the year, Coloma comes to life on its several historic demonstration days, during which visitors can view aspects of all sorts of gold-rush-era industrial and domestic life, along with period crafts. Demonstration days are spread throughout the year. Call ahead for specific dates: (916) 622-3470.

ANGELS CAMP AND CALAVERAS COUNTY

Calaveras County, of Mark Twain's jumping frog fame, has the highest concentration of historic markers of any county in California: forty-two Landmarks, four Points of Interest, and eleven entries in the National Register of Historic Places. It may also have the highest concentration of art galleries, antique shops, and bed and breakfasts as well.

This was one of the earliest, and certainly one of the most important, of the California gold-strike districts. Since 1848 nine million ounces of gold have been mined in the county. But Calaveras County is probably best known to Americans outside California for Twain's tale of a celebrated jumping frog and for the annual frog jumping contest held in Angels Camp every May.

Angels Camp is one of the chief leg-stretching sites along California 49. It is a quiet, lovely little place, unpretentious and with little to distinguish itself from other towns of its size. Except for the frogs. Frogs of every artistic ilk and hue are displayed in abundance in shop windows along Angels Camp's main street.

There is plenty to see and do in Calaveras County. In addition to its famous frog olympics, Angels Camp is the site of an annual zucchini festival and the Firemen's Fun Day. In nearby communities, other activities include a quilt fair, firemen's dance, and annual parade in Arnold; a classic car rally, a shrimp feed, the Miss Gold Country Pageant, Oktoberfest, and an annual homecoming event in Murphys; a Christmas dance, hospital bazaar, and Black Bart Days in San Andreas; Lumberjack Days in West Point; and a powwow in Snyder. The Calaveras County Fairgrounds hosts a county fair, Mark Twain Days, a junior rodeo, a crab feed, and a Christmas holiday fair. Calaveras communities also sponsor a broad assortment of arts and crafts fairs, concerts, and athletic events that include a biathalon, triathalon, foot races, and mountain bike competitions. You'll find something going on in the area nearly every weekend. For specific dates, call Calaveras County Visitors Association: 1 800 225-3764 or (209) 736-0049.

COLUMBIA STATE HISTORICAL PARK

Toward the southern end of the main gold-strike region lies Columbia, first a mining camp, then a prosperous little city, and now a historical park administered by the state of California.

Columbia was a mining center of real stature, yielding $87 million in gold. During the early 1850s Columbia could boast a population of 15,000, along with seventeen stores, eight hotels, four banks, three theaters, three churches, forty saloons, and two fire companies. There was also a daguerreotype parlor, a bowling alley, a brewery, and a Masonic Lodge. Two major fires, in 1854 and 1857, prompted rebuilding in brick, but after 1860 the mining slowed considerably and the town began its downward slide. Although Columbia never did completely die out, it had been severely depopulated for many years prior to the State's decision in 1945 to preserve the town as a historical attraction.

Today Columbia has stagecoach rides, an ice-cream parlor, panning for gold, saloons that advertise "kids and ladies welcome," and dance-hall girls. It also has two restored hotels: the City Hotel, in 1860s' trim; and the Fallon Hotel, restored to 1890s' standards. The old Fallon Theater, site of summer repertory since 1951, was restored in the mid-eighties at a cost of $3.5 million.

Columbia is a real-life town where people actually do live in private residences. But it is also a period piece, a living museum faithfully restored to the look of its heyday in the early 1860s.

More to do in Gold Country

In addition to the many historic sites along this scenic highway, there's an abundance of recreational opportunities as well: fishing, camping, hiking, boating, rafting (several whitewater outfitters operate along the American River), and the always-popular gold panning.

PLACERVILLE TO SACRAMENTO

The Pony Express route between Sacramento and Placerville varied greatly from time to time. What had been a straightforward ride of forty-five miles for the Pony Express in 1860 is today something of a conundrum for those intent on retracing as closely as possible the original trail. Because the countryside between Placerville and Sacramento has been so heavily developed in recent years, the precise route (actually, the lack of a precise route) is further obscured.

For the first three months of the service, the Pony Express followed a route just to the south of US 50, from Sacramento to Placerville. In July of 1860, when Folsom became the western terminus, riders switched to the northern route through Pleasant Grove.

Return to US 50 for the drive to Folsom; or, to visit the site of Pleasant Grove House remount station, exit US 50 at Cameron Park Road and drive north 3.2 miles to the intersection with Green Valley Road. Across this intersection, note the familiar Pony Express monument. Turn left (west) and drive 1.4 miles to Pleasant Grove House, obvious on the right. The house is a private residence, but there is a group of three monuments on the roadside.

You can continue on Green Valley Road into Folsom. Just where the housing subdivisions make the suburbs of Folsom really obvious, Green Valley Road intersects East Natoma and Blue Ravine roads. Follow Natoma into town to where it ends at Folsom Boulevard. Turn right, and immediately find yourself at Sutter Street, the nicely preserved Folsom oldtown.

FOLSOM

(all services)

Starting July 1, 1860, Folsom succeeded Sacramento as the western terminus for the riders, when it was deemed easier to place the Pony Express mail on the regular trains from here to Sacramento. This lasted till July 1, 1861, when Placerville became the riders' westernmost stop.

There's plenty to see in Folsom, and your visit should start at the Folsom History Museum, in the Sutter Street historic district, where you will also find nearly 150 arts and antiques shops and over twenty restaurants. The Museum is housed in the original Wells Fargo building, which was also home to the Pony Express (open Wednesday through Sunday, 11 a.m. to 4 p.m.; free admission). Here you will find complete information on Folsom's history and other attractions, including the unique Folsom Prison Museum and prisoner-run crafts shop.

From Folsom, drive twenty-five miles to the end of the trail at Sacramento, either on US 50 or on the old highway (Folsom Boulevard).

Nothing remains of Fifteen Mile House, though the site is about 0.4 mile east of the fork of White Rock Road.

If you enter Sacramento on Folsom Boulevard, you might notice the bar and pool parlor called Perkins Station on the south side of the road, 0.5 mile west of Florin-Perkins Road. In spite of the prominent Pony Express logo on the building (and regardless of claims to the contrary by the nice folks inside), this establishment had nothing to do with the Pony Express. It is, however, a friendly, respectable place to shoot pool....

Five Mile House was about 0.5 mile north of US 50, 0.6 mile west of Perkins, about 1,000 feet upstream on the Sacramento River from Alumni Grove at Sacramento State University.

Sutter Street, Folsom, California.

SACRAMENTO

(all services)

In 1839 a Swiss immigrant named John Sutter built a fort and trading post on the banks of the American River, intent on attracting European settlers to what he foresaw as an agriculture empire. Sutter's small enterprise grew steadily, till, in 1848, he decided to finance a sawmill farther up the river.

It was the accidental discovery of gold by Sutter's foreman, James Marshall, that sparked Sacramento's meteoric growth. Commercial enterprises sprouted all along the riverfront as the small community expanded to accommodate the needs of growing numbers of prospectors flocking to the diggings in the nearby hills. John Sutter appears to have been rather less than enthusiastic about the unforseen boom. He turned his land and commercial ventures over to his son, who promptly subdivided the land in proper western real-estate development style, and named the new city Sacramento.

The rapid influx of gold-seekers and camp followers in the two years after the initial strikes led to California's admittance to the Union in 1850. Due to its important situation as the economic, social, and political hub of the growing gold-strike districts, Sacramento was named capital in 1854.

David Rosen demonstrates an old printing press at a Pony Express exhibit in old Sacramento.

By the time of the Pony Express, Sacramento was a thriving community of real substance. A twenty-eight-acre portion of what was once the heart of the original city along the riverfront has been restored to its original condition. This important historic and tourist district, called Old Sacramento, boasts the largest concentration of restored historic buildings in the entire state.

The office of the Alta Telegraph Company served as the original western terminus for the Pony Express route. Today this office has been largely restored to period appearance as a California State Parks museum. Look for it in the B.F. Hastings Building, adjacent to the prominent Pony Express statue at Second and J streets in Old Sacramento.

Old Sacramento is also the site of the California State Railroad Museum, one of the best interpretive railroad museums in the entire world.

Sutter's Fort is about 1.5 miles east of Old Sacramento, at 27th and L streets. Special exhibits include blacksmith and cooper shops, a prison, a bakery, and restored living and livestock areas. It's open daily, 10 a.m. to 5 p.m. Admission for adults is $2, kids 6-12 $1.

Visitor Information Center (open daily, 9 a.m. to 5 p.m.), 1104 Front St., in Old Sacramento; (916) 264-7777 (Monday through Friday); (916) 442-7644 (weekends).

Joe Bensen, lost in the Nevada desert.

ABOUT THE AUTHOR

In 1990 Joe Bensen started his own writing and photography business, WORLDPIX. His credits include numerous magazine articles on such diverse subjects as mountain sports and adventure travel, American popular culture, and the White Separatist movement. Prior to founding WORLDPIX, he spent two years as a wire-service news photographer, working out of the Reuters East Africa bureau.

Bensen is co-author (with Randall Green) of *Bugaboo Rock: A Climber's Guide to the Bugaboo Range* (Mountaineers, 1990), and co-author (with Robert Silberman) and photographer of a work in progress on current conditions in former mining communities of the American West.

Bensen received his BA in English Literature from Purdue University (1971) and his MA in Visual Communication from the University of Minnesota (1985), where he taught photojournalism from 1984 to 1988. He currently lives in the Phoenix, Arizona, area, where he is pursuing an MFA in the School of Art at Arizona State University.

Out Here there's No One to Ask Directions

Let Falcon Be Your Guide

The **FALCON**GUIDES series consists of recreational guidebooks designed to help you safely enjoy the great outdoors. Each 6 x 9" softcover book features up-to-date maps, photos, and detailed information on access, hazards, side trips, special attractions, and more. So whether you're planning you first adventure or have enjoyed the outdoors for years, a **FALCON**GUIDE makes an ideal companion.

For more information about these and other Falcon Press books, please visit your local bookstore, or call or write for a free catalog.

Falcon Press • P.O. Box 1718 • Helena, Montana 59624
1-800-582-2665

FALCON™

FALCONGUIDES *Perfect for every outdoor adventure!*

FISHING
Angler's Guide to Alaska
Angler's Guide to Montana

FLOATING
Floater's Guide to Colorado
Floater's Guide to Missouri
Floater's Guide to Montana

HIKING
Hiker's Guide to Alaska
Hiker's Guide to Alberta
Hiker's Guide to Arizona
Hiker's Guide to California
Hiker's Guide to Colorado
Hiker's Guide to Florida
Hiker's Guide to Georgia
Hiker's Guide to Hot Springs
  in the Pacific Northwest
Hiker's Guide to Idaho
Hiker's Guide to Montana
Hiker's Guide to Montana's
  Continental Divide Trail
Hiker's Guide to Nevada
Hiker's Guide to New Mexico
Hiker's Guide to North Carolina
Hiker's Guide to Oregon
Hiker's Guide to Texas
Hiker's Guide to Utah
Hiker's Guide to Virginia
Hiker's Guide to Washington
Hiker's Guide to Wyoming
Trail Guide to Glacier/Waterton
  National Parks
Wild Country Companion

MOUNTAIN BIKING
Mountain Biker's Guide to Arizona
Mountain Biker's Guide to
  Central Appalachia
Mountain Biker's Guide to Colorado
Mountain Biker's Guide to New Mexico
Mountain Biker's Guide to Northern
  California/Nevada
Mountain Biker's Guide to Northern
  New England
Mountain Biker's Guide to the
  Northern Rockies
Mountain Biker's Guide to the Ozarks

Mountain Biker's Guide to
  the Southeast
Mountain Biker's Guide to
  Southern California
Mountain Biker's Guide to Southern
  New England

ROCKHOUNDING
Rockhound's Guide to Arizona
Rockhound's Guide to Montana

SCENIC DRIVING
Arizona Scenic Drives
Back Country Byways
California Scenic Drives
Colorado Scenic Drives
New Mexico Scenic Drives
Oregon Scenic Drives
Scenic Byways
Scenic Byways II
Trail of the Great Bear
Traveler's Guide to the Oregon Trail
Traveler's Guide to the
  Lewis and Clark Trail

WILDLIFE VIEWING GUIDES
Arizona Wildlife Viewing Guide
California Wildlife Viewing Guide
Colorado Wildlife Viewing Guide
Florida Wildlife Viewing Guide
Idaho Wildlife Viewing Guide
Indiana Wildlife Viewing Guide
Montana Wildlife Viewing Guide
Nevada Wildlife Viewing Guide
New Mexico Wildlife Viewing Guide
North Carolina Wildlife Viewing Guide
North Dakota Wildlife Viewing Guide
Oregon Wildlife Viewing Guide
Tennessee Wildlife Viewing Guide
Texas Wildlife Viewing Guide
Utah Wildlife Viewing Guide
Washington Wildlife Viewing Guide

PLUS—
Birder's Guide to Montana
Hunter's Guide to Montana
Recreation Guide to
  California National Forests
Recreation Guide to Washington
  National Forests

BRING ALONG A COMPANION

On your next trip to the great outdoors, bring along our FalconGuide, *Wild Country Companion*. Learn indispensable state-of-the-art methods for safe, no-trace traveling in North America's backcountry—whether you're on foot, bike or horse.

This guide was carefully compiled from recommendations by a range of experts including Forest Service researchers and managers, rangers, guides, and outdoor school instructors. It is packed with indispensible information on how to safely deal with hazards from bugs to bears and provides specific methods on different some regions. There's also plenty of interesting anecdotes and illustrations.

As more and more people take to the outdoors, *Wild Country Companion* offers new ways to sustain our recreation resources. This book goes hand-in-hand with all our other FalconGuides and is a must for outdoor enthusiasts.

WILD COUNTRY COMPANION

By Will Harmon, Illustrated by Lisa Harvey
160 pp., 6 x 9", charts, softcover

FALCON™